OR

Is It a Game or Is It Life?

ARTHUR SCHECHTER
OR PAULA SCHECHTER

Andrews McMeel
Publishing

Kansas City

00 01 02 03 04 BIN 10 9 8 7 6 5 4 3 2 1

Library of Congress Cataloging-in-Publication Data
Schechter, Arthur.
   Or : is it a game or is it life? / by Arthur Schechter or Paula
   Schechter.
       p. cm.
   ISBN 0-7407-1022-2 (pbk.)
   1. Choice (Psychology)—Miscellanea. I. Schechter, Paula. II.
Title.

BF611.S34 2000
081—dc21   00-044210

Book design by Holly Camerlinck

Contents

Preface

"Thus he will seek to understand what is in effect,
for good *or* evil, of beauty combined with wealth *or*
with poverty and with this *or* that condition of the
soul, *or* of any combination of high *or* low birth, public *or* private station, strength *or* weakness, quickness
of wit *or* slowness, and any other qualities of mind,
native *or* acquired; until, as the outcome of all these
calculations, he is able to choose between the worse
and the better life with reference to the constitution
of the soul, calling a life worse *or* better according as
it leads to the soul becoming more unjust *or* more
just. All else he will leave out of account, for, as he
have seen, this is the supreme choice for a man, both
while he lives and after death."

—PLATO, *THE REPUBLIC*, CHAPTER X, "THE MYTH OF ER"

OR

"When you come to the fork in the road, take it."

—YOGI BERRA

Acknowledgments

Our heartfelt thanks to dear family and friends who added greatly to the creative process

OR

Just wanted to get their names in our book:

Martin Arnold; Nancy Beaubaire; Robert Bees; Laura and Rich Bernstein; Natalie and Harvey Cohen; Wendy Coppolla; Julie and Brad Ellis; Kelly Ellston; Howie and Paula Entin; Liz and Andy Hirtenstein; Kit Johnson; Shari, Abbi, and Ariel Jutkowitz; Ilene Madwed; Carol Mann-Cohen; Faith, Jorge, Jeremy, and Anthony Morfa; David, Lisa, Joshua, and Halle Neisen; Lisa Orthman; Marc Peyser; Isabel Rodriguez; Debbie and Robert Rosenblum; Lisa Stein; Susan Stelmach; Steve, Dorothy, Josh, and Nolan Zeide.

A User's Guide
OR
Introduction

Is It a Game or Is It Life?

One day while driving to our favorite Chinese restaurant my newlywed wife barraged me with inane questions about love, fidelity, and implausible what-ifs. To return the favor, I responded with a few totally unrelated and irrelevant questions of my own:

William Hurt *or* William Shakespeare?
Paper *or* Plastic?
Batman *or* Superman?

And with that retort *OR* was born.

OR is a book about choices, opinions, feelings, and preferences—the kind we make every day in our lives, like diet *or* exercise. And it's about the kind of choices we hope we never have to make, like tell your friend their spouse is unfaithful *or* keep your mouth shut. Also, *OR* raises combinations of hypothetical choices. These don't really come up in life, but your selection reveals so much—like tax audit *or* rectal exam.

OR enables us to explore ourselves as well as others by examining our values, experiences, dreams, and desires. Lightheartedly, pros and cons are weighed as *OR* stimulates conversation on a wide variety of topics from the serious to the sublime.

Discussing the book offers insight on morals, personality, and humor. *OR* tests your knowledge of pop culture, history, politics, science, sports, and people. It gives you the chance to learn inner thoughts about your mate, your friends, your family, and your coworkers.

To "play," simply select an "*OR*" and ask others to choose one *or* the other. The fun part is the discussion that follows. You merely explain the merit considered when deciding on your preference. What criteria were factored in: popularity, accomplishments, contribution to mankind, values, or with whom do you identify?

Playing in a group and want to keep score? One way is to award a point for each time both partners in a team correctly predict what the other will pick. Or make up your own scoring.

We suggest OR as a primer for the conversationally challenged or the party animal and recommend the book on dates, at parties, in a classroom, on car rides, and in sports bars. Try OR even for those solitary moments in the bathroom. Different settings and people will help determine which chapters to explore.

In many cases you might not wish to choose either option of a specific OR. But play the game. Choose one, even if your choice is the lesser of two evils or the better of two favorites.

Most of all, remember there is no right *or* wrong answer.

The Classics

OR

The Originals

Coffee **OR** *Tea*

■ ■ ■

Boy **OR** *Girl*

■ ■ ■

Coke **OR** *Pepsi*

■ ■ ■

Smoking **OR** *Nonsmoking*

■ ■ ■

AC **OR** *DC*

■ ■ ■

Boxers **OR** *Briefs*

■ ■ ■

Cat **OR** *Dog*

Mary Ann **OR** *Ginger*

■ ■ ■

Big Bang Theory **OR** *Evolution*

■ ■ ■

Nature **OR** *Nurture*

■ ■ ■

Brains **OR** *Brawn*

■ ■ ■

Paper **OR** *Plastic*

■ ■ ■

M&M's: Plain **OR** *Peanut*

Truth **OR** *Dare*

■ ■ ■

Trick **OR** *Treat*

■ ■ ■

Wash **OR** *Dry*

■ ■ ■

Single **OR** *Married*

■ ■ ■

Which Came First:
The Chicken **OR** *The Egg*

■ ■ ■

Pro-Life **OR** *Pro-Choice*

Heads **OR** *Tails*

■ ■ ■

Odds **OR** *Evens*

■ ■ ■

Wholesale **OR** *Retail*

■ ■ ■

Death Penalty **OR** *Life in Prison*

■ ■ ■

Tastes Great **OR** *Less Filling*

■ ■ ■

Mounds **OR** *Almond Joy*

Cash **OR** *Credit*

■ ■ ■

President Kennedy's Assassination:
Conspiracy **OR** *Single Bullet*

■ ■ ■

Lucky **OR** *Good*

■ ■ ■

Window **OR** *Aisle*

■ ■ ■

Fact **OR** *Fiction*

■ ■ ■

Half Full **OR** *Half Empty*

Beat 'Em **OR** *Join 'Em*

■ ■ ■

Love 'Em **OR** *Leave 'Em*

■ ■ ■

Lucky at Love **OR** *Lucky at Cards*

■ ■ ■

Bottle **OR** *Can*

■ ■ ■

Shower **OR** *Bath*

■ ■ ■

Pen **OR** *Pencil*

■ ■ ■

Sugar: One Lump **OR** *Two*

Elevator **OR** *Stairs*

■ ■ ■

Show **OR** *Tell*

■ ■ ■

Wine: Red **OR** *White*

■ ■ ■

Quantity **OR** *Quality*

■ ■ ■

Your Place **OR** *Mine*

■ ■ ■

Hamburger **OR** *Hot Dog*

■ ■ ■

Ketchup **OR** *Mustard*

Sex

OR

Dating

Internet Chat Room OR

Newspaper Personals

■　■　■

Elope OR Big Family Ceremony

■　■　■

Condom OR The Pill

■　■　■

First Date: Kiss OR Kiss Off

■　■　■

Dutch Treat OR My Treat

■　■　■

Hard to Get OR Easy

Virgin **OR** *Experienced*

. . .

Feminism **OR** *Chivalry*

. . .

Pregnancy Test: Positive **OR** *Negative*

. . .

One Night Stand **OR** *Commitment*

. . .

Double Date **OR** *Blind Date*

. . .

Call to Cancel **OR** *Stand Up*

. . .

Breast Implants **OR** *Breast Reduction*

Loved and Lost OR

Never to Have Loved at All

■ ■ ■

Unhappy Marriage OR *Divorce*

■ ■ ■

Edible Underwear OR *No Underwear*

■ ■ ■

Crotchless Panties OR *G-String*

■ ■ ■

A Cup OR *DDD Cup*

■ ■ ■

Soft Body Woman OR *Muscular Woman*

Man's Chest: Hairy **OR** *Bare*

■ ■ ■

Interracial Marriage **OR** *Interfaith Marriage*

■ ■ ■

Sex in the Car **OR** *Sex in the Outdoors*

■ ■ ■

Spouse: Snores in Bed **OR** *Insomnia*

■ ■ ■

Circumcised **OR** *Uncircumcised*

■ ■ ■

Bachelorette Party **OR** *Shower*

■ ■ ■

Orgy **OR** *Celibacy*

The Joy of Sex OR The Kama Sutra

■ ■ ■

Teddy OR *Garter Belt*

■ ■ ■

Exhibitionist OR *Prude*

■ ■ ■

Nudist Camp OR *Topless Beach*

■ ■ ■

Move in with Mother-in-law OR
Mother-in-law Moves in with You

■ ■ ■

Partner: Younger OR *Older*

Sex in the Morning **OR** *Sex at Night*

■ ■ ■

Vasectomy **OR** *Tie Tubes*

■ ■ ■

Watch an Adult Video **OR**
Be in an Adult Video

■ ■ ■

Guy Ask Girl on Date **OR**
Girl Ask Guy on Date

■ ■ ■

Physical Love **OR** *Emotional Love*

■ ■ ■

Sex Education: School **OR** *Home*

Get Married **OR** *Live Together*

■ ■ ■

Spin the Bottle **OR** *Post Office*

■ ■ ■

Dominant **OR** *Submissive*

■ ■ ■

Naughty **OR** *Nice*

■ ■ ■

Mate's Little Black Book: Read **OR** *Let It Be*

■ ■ ■

Divorced with Child, Lover:
Spends the Night **OR** *Must Go Home*

Discover Spouse Is Bisexual:
Love 'Em **OR** *Leave 'Em*

■ ■ ■

Dating Boss May Lead to:
Problem **OR** *Career Advancement*

■ ■ ■

Long-Distance Relationship:
Wrong Number **OR** *Call May Go Through*

■ ■ ■

Age Daughter May Begin Dating:
Twelve **OR** *Fifteen*

■ ■ ■

Spouse Has Affair: Forgive **OR** *Leave*

First Date: *Single Rose* **OR** *Bouquet of Roses*

■ ■ ■

Mate's Valentine's Day Gift:
Chocolate **OR** *Flowers*

■ ■ ■

Bad Boy **OR** *Good Boy*

■ ■ ■

Age to Get Married: Twenty **OR** *Forty*

■ ■ ■

During Sex: Lights On **OR** *Lights Off*

■ ■ ■

Ex: Remain Friends **OR** *Out of the Picture*

Cybersex **OR** *Real Sex*

■ ■ ■

Size Does Matter **OR** *Size Doesn't Matter*

■ ■ ■

Use of Sexuality: Cheapens **OR** *Empowers*

■ ■ ■

Models in Adult Magazines:
Nude **OR** *With Lingerie*

■ ■ ■

Impotence Cure: Viagra **OR** *Penile Implant*

■ ■ ■

Back Massage **OR** *Foot Massage*

Herpes **OR** *Venereal Disease*

■ ■ ■

A Good Night's Entertainment:
Watch TV **OR** *Make Love*

■ ■ ■

The Way to a Man's Heart
Is Through His Stomach: True **OR** *False*

■ ■ ■

Underwear Style:
Wearer's Preference **OR** *Partner's Preference*

■ ■ ■

Die First: Spouse **OR** *Self*

Traits

OR

Personalities

World Peace OR *Personal Wealth*

■ ■ ■

Pray OR *Cross Your Fingers*

■ ■ ■

Tough Chick OR *Damsel in Distress*

■ ■ ■

Careful OR *Carefree*

■ ■ ■

Outer Beauty OR *Inner Substance*

■ ■ ■

Early Bird OR *Night Owl*

■ ■ ■

Obsessive-Compulsive OR *Anal Retentive*

Live Forever **OR** *End World Hunger*

∎ ∎ ∎

Poor **OR** *Stupid*

∎ ∎ ∎

Richest Person Alive **OR** *Sexiest Person Alive*

∎ ∎ ∎

Bald **OR** *Fat*

∎ ∎ ∎

Anonymous **OR** *Famous*

∎ ∎ ∎

Atheist **OR** *Belief in God*

∎ ∎ ∎

Activist **OR** *Pacifist*

Midget **OR** *Giant*

■ ■ ■

Phony **OR** *Dumb*

■ ■ ■

Behind the Scenes **OR** *In Front of the Camera*

■ ■ ■

Happy **OR** *Successful*

■ ■ ■

Simple **OR** *Complex*

■ ■ ■

Old-Fashioned **OR** *Modern*

■ ■ ■

Diet **OR** *Exercise*

Return Shopping Cart **OR**
Leave in Parking Lot

■ ■ ■

Symbolism **OR** Substance

■ ■ ■

Humorless **OR** Smart Aleck

■ ■ ■

Feel Good **OR** Look Good

■ ■ ■

Right Brain **OR** Left Brain

■ ■ ■

Bad Food: Send Back **OR** Eat

Bad Service: Tip **OR** *Stiff*

■ ■ ■

Bigot **OR** *Insane*

■ ■ ■

My Way **OR** *The Highway*

■ ■ ■

Introverted **OR** *Extroverted*

■ ■ ■

Creature of Habit **OR** *Spontaneous*

■ ■ ■

Type A Personality **OR** *Type B Personality*

■ ■ ■

Loyal **OR** *Responsible*

Healthy **OR** *Wealthy*

■ ■ ■

Truth **OR** *Consequences*

■ ■ ■

Public Speaking **OR** *Pet a Snake*

■ ■ ■

Fear of Flying **OR** *Arachnophobia*

■ ■ ■

Optimist **OR** *Pessimist*

■ ■ ■

Read the Directions **OR** *Dive In*

Big Fish in Small Pond OR
Small Fish in Big Pond

■ ■ ■

Vengeance OR *Forgiveness*

■ ■ ■

Set Watch: Five Minutes Fast OR
On Time

■ ■ ■

Look Young OR *Feel Young*

■ ■ ■

Tomboy OR *Daddy's Girl*

■ ■ ■

Brutally Honest OR *Tell a White Lie*

Spend **OR** *Save*

■ ■ ■

Weekend: Relax on Couch **OR** *Active*

■ ■ ■

Scream and Let It Out **OR** *Keep It Inside*

■ ■ ■

Homosexuality: Born **OR** *Acquired*

■ ■ ■

Concrete **OR** *Abstract*

■ ■ ■

Follow **OR** *Lead*

■ ■ ■

Street Smart **OR** *Book Smart*

Peacemaker OR *Judge*

■   ■   ■

Sympathetic OR *Callous*

■   ■   ■

Practical OR *Frivolous*

■   ■   ■

Rule with: Your Head OR *Your Heart*

■   ■   ■

Live Long OR *Live Fast*

■   ■   ■

Routine Activity OR *Adventure*

■   ■   ■

Judging OR *Perceiving*

See Someone Shoplift:

Tell Store Owner **OR** *Mind Your Business*

■ ■ ■

Good News and Bad News, Hear First:

Good News **OR** *Bad News*

■ ■ ■

Actor in Police Drama:

Good Cop **OR** *Bad Cop*

■ ■ ■

Pretty Face **OR** *Pretty Body*

■ ■ ■

Bully Wants to Fight:

Duke It Out **OR** *Talk It Out*

Watch **OR** *Do*

. . .

Talk to Plants **OR** *Talk to Yourself*

. . .

Daring **OR** *Cautious*

. . .

Giver **OR** *Taker*

. . .

Tickle **OR** *Be Tickled*

. . .

People Are Basically: Good **OR** *Evil*

. . .

Angel **OR** *Devil*

Sports

OR

Fitness

Pete Rose **OR** *Ty Cobb*

■ ■ ■

Ted Williams **OR** *Joe DiMaggio*

■ ■ ■

Artificial Turf **OR** *Grass*

■ ■ ■

NASCAR **OR** *Indy Car*

■ ■ ■

Marathon **OR** *100-Yard Dash*

■ ■ ■

Muhammed Ali **OR** *Joe Frazier*

Wilt Chamberlain **OR** *Bill Russell*

■ ■ ■

Golf **OR** *Tennis*

■ ■ ■

Winter Olympics **OR** *Summer Olympics*

■ ■ ■

Jim Brown **OR** *Barry Sanders*

■ ■ ■

Dan Marino **OR** *Joe Montana*

■ ■ ■

Wayne Gretzky **OR** *Mario Lemieux*

Greg Maddux **OR** Nolan Ryan

■ ■ ■

Larry Bird **OR** Magic Johnson

■ ■ ■

Ken Griffey, Jr. **OR** Barry Bonds

■ ■ ■

Offense **OR** Defense

■ ■ ■

Pro Football:

Instant Replay **OR** Referee Decision

■ ■ ■

Box Seats **OR** Bleachers

Tiger Woods **OR** Jack Nicklaus

■ ■ ■

Lose a Blowout **OR** Lose a Nail-biter

■ ■ ■

NCAA Football: Bowl Championship Series
OR Polls Determine Who's #1

■ ■ ■

George Steinbrenner **OR** Al Davis

■ ■ ■

Roger Clemens **OR** Randy Johnson

■ ■ ■

Sugar Ray Leonard **OR** Marvin Hagler

Babe Didrickson Zaharias **OR**

Jackie Joyner-Kersee

∎ ∎ ∎

Babe Ruth **OR** *Willie Mays*

∎ ∎ ∎

Charles Barkley:
Big Talent **OR** *Big Mouth*

∎ ∎ ∎

Albert Belle: Slugger **OR** *Slug*

∎ ∎ ∎

Dennis Rodman:
Hall of Fame **OR** *Hall of Shame*

Rickey Henderson **OR** *Lou Brock*

■ ■ ■

Bobby Knight: Coach **OR** *Intimidator*

■ ■ ■

Salary Cap **OR** *Unlimited Money*

■ ■ ■

David Stern **OR** *Pete Rozelle*

■ ■ ■

Tommy Lasorda **OR** *Sparky Anderson*

■ ■ ■

Chris Evert **OR** *Martina Navratilova*

■ ■ ■

John McEnroe **OR** *Jimmy Connors*

OR
40

Carl Lewis OR Jesse Owens

■ ■ ■

Dick Butkus OR Lawrence Taylor

■ ■ ■

Vince Lombardi OR Don Shula

■ ■ ■

John Stockton OR Bob Cousy

■ ■ ■

Designated Hitter OR Pitcher Bats

■ ■ ■

Jim Palmer OR Tom Seaver

■ ■ ■

Lou Gehrig OR Cal Ripken, Jr.

Mike Schmidt **OR** George Brett

■ ■ ■

Jeff Gordon **OR** Dale Earnhardt

■ ■ ■

Sports Talk Radio:
Turn-On **OR** Turnoff

■ ■ ■

Best Athlete of Twentieth Century:
Jim Thorpe **OR** Michael Jordan

■ ■ ■

Joe Namath **OR** Johnny Unitas

■ ■ ■

Miracle on Ice **OR** Miracle Mets

Latrell Sprewell **OR** P. J. Carlesimo

■ ■ ■

Tony Gwynn **OR** Wade Boggs

■ ■ ■

Pro Basketball **OR** College Basketball

■ ■ ■

Pro Football **OR** College Football

■ ■ ■

Bo Jackson **OR** Deion Sanders

■ ■ ■

Paul "Bear" Bryant **OR** Eddie Robinson

■ ■ ■

Pete Sampras **OR** Andre Agassi

Penny Hardaway OR *Tim Hardaway*

■ ■ ■

Sports Illustrated *Swimsuit Issue:*
Out of This World OR *Out of Place*

■ ■ ■

Joe Louis OR *Jack Dempsey*

■ ■ ■

Baseball Hall of Fame:
Watershed Mark OR *Watered-Down*

■ ■ ■

Olga Korbut OR *Nadia Comaneci*

■ ■ ■

Bill Walsh OR *Bill Parcells*

David Robinson **OR** *Hakeem Olajuwon*

■ ■ ■

John Elway **OR** *Brett Favre*

■ ■ ■

Baseball Interleague Play:
Great Innovation **OR** *Breaks Tradition*

■ ■ ■

Athletes:
Role Models **OR** *Just Talented Players*

■ ■ ■

Steve Young **OR** *Troy Aikman*

■ ■ ■

Evander Holyfield **OR** *Mike Tyson*

Michael Irvin **OR** *Cris Carter*

■   ■   ■

Dome Stadiums:
A Necessary Evil **OR** *Just Evil*

■   ■   ■

Mike Piazza **OR** *Ivan Rodriguez*

■   ■   ■

Mark McGwire **OR** *Sammy Sosa*

■   ■   ■

Venus Williams **OR** *Serena Williams*

■   ■   ■

Olympic Spirit:
Alive and Well **OR** *Dead and Buried*

Women Journalists in Men's Locker Room:
Yea **OR** Nay

■ ■ ■

Win NIT **OR**
Lose in First Round of NCAA

■ ■ ■

Sports: Business **OR** Game

■ ■ ■

Nomar Garciaparra **OR** Derek Jeter

■ ■ ■

Phil Jackson **OR** Pat Riley

■ ■ ■

Chipper Jones **OR** Matt Williams

Nancy Kerrigan **OR** *Tonya Harding*

■   ■   ■

Bodybuilding Contests: Fitness Celebration
OR *Just a Little Weird*

■   ■   ■

Girls in Little League: Fair **OR** *Foul*

■   ■   ■

Curt Schilling **OR** *Orel Hershiser*

■   ■   ■

Good Field/No Hit **OR** *Good Hit/No Field*

■   ■   ■

Leon Spinks **OR** *Michael Spinks*

Baseball **OR** *Football*

■   ■   ■

Moses Malone **OR** *Robert Parish*

■   ■   ■

George Foreman: Fat **OR** *Phat*

■   ■   ■

Andre Dawson **OR** *Dave Winfield*

■   ■   ■

Johnny Bench **OR** *Carlton Fisk*

■   ■   ■

Length of Baseball Game:
Speed Up **OR** *Don't Mess with Perfection*

Free Agency: Killing Sports **OR**
It's the American Way

■ ■ ■

Attend: Minor League Game **OR**
Major League Game

■ ■ ■

Darryl Strawberry's Legacy:
Home-Run Hitter **OR** *Unfulfilled Potential*

■ ■ ■

Fitness Shows on TV:
Watch Girls **OR** *Exercise*

Sports Agents:
Necessary in Today's World **OR** *Pond Scum*

■ ■ ■

Moises Alou **OR** *David Justice*

■ ■ ■

Dwight Gooden's Legacy:
Dr. K **OR** *Dr(un)K*

■ ■ ■

Mike Holmgren **OR** *Mike Shanahan*

■ ■ ■

Side with in Sports Strikes:
Players **OR** *Owners*

Alonzo Mourning **OR** *Patrick Ewing*

■ ■ ■

After Scoring Touchdown: Celebrate **OR**
Behave Like You've Scored Before

■ ■ ■

Running Back **OR** *Quarterback*

■ ■ ■

Stephon Marbury **OR** *Allen Iverson*

■ ■ ■

Peggy Fleming **OR** *Dorothy Hamill*

■ ■ ■

Red Auerbach **OR** *Lenny Wilkens*

Keith Hernandez **OR** Don Mattingly

■ ■ ■

WWF **OR** *WCW*

■ ■ ■

Tennis: Singles **OR** *Doubles*

■ ■ ■

Pro Wrestling: Sport **OR** *Entertainment*

■ ■ ■

Jerry Rice **OR** *Art Monk*

■ ■ ■

Tom Glavine **OR** *John Smoltz*

■ ■ ■

Bob Costas **OR** *Al Michaels*

American League **OR** *National League*

■ ■ ■

Kentucky Derby **OR** *Indianapolis 500*

■ ■ ■

U.S. Olympic Basketball:
NBA Dream Team **OR** *College Kids*

■ ■ ■

Track **OR** *Field*

■ ■ ■

Love Handles **OR** *Cottage Cheese Thighs*

■ ■ ■

Bill Shoemaker **OR** *Laffit Pincay, Jr.*

Sex Before Athletic Event:
Enhances Performance **OR**
Hinders Performance

■ ■ ■

Soccer **OR** *Hockey*

■ ■ ■

Monday Night Football:
Best Game in Town **OR**
Not What It Used to Be

■ ■ ■

Bernie Williams **OR** *Kenny Lofton*

■ ■ ■

Jeff Bagwell **OR** *Mo Vaughn*

MLB Umpires Revolt:
Good Arbitrators Lost **OR** *Good Riddance*

■ ■ ■

John Rocker's Legacy:
Reliever **OR** *Redneck*

■ ■ ■

Fenway Park **OR** *Camden Yards*

■ ■ ■

Earl Weaver **OR** *Billy Martin*

■ ■ ■

Bobby Hull **OR** *Brett Hull*

■ ■ ■

Andruw Jones **OR** *Vladimir Guerrero*

Carl Yastrzemski **OR** *Stan Musial*

■ ■ ■

Dan Fouts **OR** *Ken Stabler*

■ ■ ■

Paul Hornung **OR** *Gale Sayers*

■ ■ ■

Phil Simms **OR** *Joe Theismann*

■ ■ ■

Sandy Koufax **OR** *Juan Marichal*

■ ■ ■

David Duval **OR** *Mark O'Meara*

■ ■ ■

Kobe Bryant **OR** *Kevin Garnett*

Politics

OR

Politicians

Liberal **OR** *Conservative*

■ ■ ■

State Rights **OR** *Federal Rights*

■ ■ ■

Welfare **OR** *No Fare*

■ ■ ■

Senator **OR**
Member of House of Representatives

■ ■ ■

Socialism **OR** *Capitalism*

■ ■ ■

Politically Correct **OR** *Politically Incorrect*

Socialized Medicine **OR** *HMO*

■ ■ ■

Hawk **OR** *Dove*

■ ■ ■

Vice President **OR** *Member of Cabinet*

■ ■ ■

Secretary of State **OR** *Attorney General*

■ ■ ■

FBI **OR** *CIA*

■ ■ ■

Jesse Jackson **OR** *Jesse Helms*

■ ■ ■

Gun Control **OR** *NRA*

Nuclear Weapons OR No Nukes

■ ■ ■

Presidential Terms: Two OR Unlimited

■ ■ ■

Gays in Military OR Women in Combat

■ ■ ■

J. Edgar Hoover OR Jimmy Hoffa

■ ■ ■

John F. Kennedy OR Robert Kennedy

■ ■ ■

Watergate OR Interngate

■ ■ ■

Karl Marx OR Vladimir Lenin

Mikhail Gorbachev **OR** *Boris Yeltsin*

■ ■ ■

James Carville **OR** *Mary Matlin*

■ ■ ■

Ross Perot **OR** *Colin Powell*

■ ■ ■

Bill Clinton **OR** *Hillary Clinton*

■ ■ ■

Legalize Pot **OR** *Legalize Prostitution*

■ ■ ■

Muammar al-Qaddafi **OR** *Saddam Hussein*

"The Star-Spangled Banner" OR
"America the Beautiful"

■ ■ ■

Martin Luther King, Jr. OR
Mahatma Gandhi

■ ■ ■

Political Action Group OR *Lobbyist*

■ ■ ■

Aaron Burr OR *Alexander Hamilton*

■ ■ ■

Big Government OR *Small Government*

Peace in Middle East: U.S. Intervention OR
Let Them Fend for Themselves

■   ■   ■

Al Gore OR *George W. Bush*

■   ■   ■

Richard Nixon OR *Spiro Agnew*

■   ■   ■

Rush Limbaugh: Right On OR
Right of Center

■   ■   ■

Yassar Arafat's Legacy:
PLO Leader OR *Terrorist*

Israel: Land for Peace **OR** *Stick by Your Guns*

■ ■ ■

Fidel Castro **OR** *Mao Tse-tung*

■ ■ ■

Franklin D. Roosevelt **OR** *Teddy Roosevelt*

■ ■ ■

George Washington **OR** *Abraham Lincoln*

■ ■ ■

Budget Surplus:
Tax Cut **OR** *Government Spending*

■ ■ ■

Benedict Arnold **OR** *Jefferson Davis*

Bishop Desmond Tutu **OR** *Nelson Mandela*

■ ■ ■

Nancy Reagan **OR** *Barbara Bush*

■ ■ ■

Michael Dukakis **OR** *Walter Mondale*

■ ■ ■

Dan Quayle's Legacy:
Family Values **OR** *"Potatoe"*

■ ■ ■

Affirmative Action:
Makes Up for Past Ills **OR** *Equally Unjust*

Bill Bradley's Legacy:
Basketball Player OR Politician

■ ■ ■

Ted Kennedy's Legacy:
Chappaquiddick OR U.S. Senator

■ ■ ■

Manuel Noriega OR Ayatollah Khomeini

■ ■ ■

Adolf Hitler OR Benito Mussolini

■ ■ ■

Indira Gandhi OR Golda Meir

Puerto Rico:

U.S. Commonwealth **OR** *Fifty-first State*

■ ■ ■

Ollie North: Hero **OR** *Zero*

■ ■ ■

John Dean **OR**
Deep Throat of Watergate Scandal

■ ■ ■

Legalized Gambling:
Rolls a Seven **OR** *Snake Eyes*

■ ■ ■

Robert Dole **OR** *Elizabeth Dole*

Anwar Sadat **OR** *Menachem Begin*

■   ■   ■

John Adams **OR** *John Quincy Adams*

■   ■   ■

Strom Thurmond: Hero to Senior Citizens
OR *Too Old for Congress*

■   ■   ■

Mandatory Retirement Due to Age:
Discriminatory **OR** *Appropriate*

■   ■   ■

Executive Privilege:
Presidential Power Run Amok **OR** *Necessary*

Americans in Vietnam: Wasn't Our Fight
OR *Tried to Preserve Democracy*

∎ ∎ ∎

G. Gordon Liddy: Patriot **OR** *Criminal*

∎ ∎ ∎

Right to Vote: Privilege **OR** *Obligation*

∎ ∎ ∎

The Gettysburg Address **OR**
The Declaration of Independence

∎ ∎ ∎

Nikita Khrushchev **OR** *Leonid Brezhnev*

∎ ∎ ∎

Tip O'Neill **OR** *Newt Gingrich*

Vince Foster's Death: Murder **OR** *Suicide*

■ ■ ■

Malcolm X **OR** *Medgar Evers*

■ ■ ■

Abby Hoffman **OR** *Tom Hayden*

■ ■ ■

House Impeaches Clinton:
Based on Facts **OR** *Partisan Politics*

■ ■ ■

Ed Koch **OR** *Rudolph Giuliani*

■ ■ ■

Marion Barry's Legacy:
D.C. Mayor **OR** *Took Drugs in Office*

Women's Lib: Feminism Gone Amok **OR**
Necessary in Today's World

■   ■   ■

Restore Diplomatic Relations with Cuba:
Sí **OR** *No*

■   ■   ■

Freedom of Information **OR**
Right of Privacy

■   ■   ■

John F. Kennedy, Jr.'s Legacy:
Died in Plane Crash **OR** *George Magazine*

First in U.S.:

Black President **OR** *Woman President*

■ ■ ■

Bigger World War II Antagonist:
Germany **OR** *Japan*

■ ■ ■

Confederate Flag:
Southern Shame **OR** *Southern Heritage*

■ ■ ■

Contol of Panama Canal: U.S. **OR** *Panama*

■ ■ ■

Man Lands on Moon: Result of Cold War
OR *One Great Leap for Mankind*

Greater Military Debacle:
Custer's Last Stand **OR** *Bay of Pigs*

■   ■   ■

Greater Military Achievement:
Normandy (D-Day) **OR**
Inchon Amphibious Landing

■   ■   ■

Military Personnel: Draft **OR** *Volunteers*

■   ■   ■

City-Mandated Curfew for Teens:
Just Law **OR** *Just Awful*

■   ■   ■

Elian Gonzalez Belongs in:
America **OR** *Cuba*

Communism **OR** Fascism

■ ■ ■

Freedom of Speech **OR** Freedom of Religion

■ ■ ■

Pat Robertson **OR** Pat Buchanan

■ ■ ■

Margaret Thatcher **OR** Winston Churchill

■ ■ ■

Social Security **OR** Personal Retirement Plan

■ ■ ■

George Herbert Walker Bush's Legacy:
Gulf War **OR** "Read My Lips—
No New Taxes"

Food

OR

Cooking

Decaf **OR** Regular Coffee

■ ■ ■

Pretzels: Salted **OR** Unsalted

■ ■ ■

Low Fat **OR** High Protein

■ ■ ■

Shrimp **OR** Lobster

■ ■ ■

Eat Corn Row by Row **OR** Circular

■ ■ ■

Butter **OR** Margarine

Drink Tea from:

Mug **OR** *Cup and Saucer*

■ ■ ■

Make Dinner **OR** *Make Reservations*

■ ■ ■

Pie **OR** *Cake*

■ ■ ■

Bake **OR** *Broil*

■ ■ ■

French Fries **OR** *Onion Rings*

■ ■ ■

Wine **OR** *Beer*

Vegetarian **OR** Carnivore

■ ■ ■

Fish **OR** Fowl

■ ■ ■

Ice Cream **OR** Frozen Yogurt

■ ■ ■

On Roast Beef Sandwich:
Mayonnaise **OR** Mustard

■ ■ ■

Skim Milk **OR** Whole Milk

■ ■ ■

White Meat **OR** Dark Meat

Movie Snack: Popcorn **OR** *Candy*

■ ■ ■

Apple: Macintosh **OR** *Delicious*

■ ■ ■

Milky Way **OR** *Snickers*

■ ■ ■

Burger King **OR** *McDonald's*

■ ■ ■

Hard Candy **OR** *Gum*

■ ■ ■

Goobers **OR** *Raisinettes*

■ ■ ■

Cool Whip **OR** *Whipped Cream*

Italian Dressing **OR** *French Dressing*

■ ■ ■

Oreo: Break Open **OR** *Eat Whole*

■ ■ ■

Baking: Mix **OR** *Scratch*

■ ■ ■

Brown Rice **OR** *White Rice*

■ ■ ■

Pizza: Deep Dish **OR** *Thin Crust*

■ ■ ■

Jell-O **OR** *Pudding*

■ ■ ■

Chinese Food **OR** *Mexican Food*

Red Grapes **OR** *Green Grapes*

■ ■ ■

Egg Salad **OR** *Tuna Salad*

■ ■ ■

Chocolate Chip Cookies **OR** *Brownies*

■ ■ ■

Soup: Cup **OR** *Bowl*

■ ■ ■

Bananas **OR** *Oranges*

■ ■ ■

Salami **OR** *Bologna*

Drink Milk:

From Container **OR** *In a Glass*

■　■　■

Crushed Ice **OR** *Cubed Ice*

■　■　■

Bottled Water **OR** *Tap Water*

■　■　■

Sunflower Seeds **OR** *Pumpkin Seeds*

■　■　■

Baked Potato Topping:

Butter **OR** *Sour Cream*

■　■　■

Porterhouse Steak **OR** *Filet Mignon*

Orange Juice: Pulp **OR** *Pulp Fiction*

■ ■ ■

Peanut Butter: Smooth **OR** *Chunky*

■ ■ ■

Soup **OR** *Salad*

■ ■ ■

Coffee: Milk and Sugar **OR** *Black*

■ ■ ■

Cottage Cheese **OR** *Rice Cakes*

■ ■ ■

Hershey's **OR** *Nestlé's*

■ ■ ■

Chocolate: With Nuts **OR** *Plain*

Hot Cereal **OR** Cold Cereal

■ ■ ■

Plain Cone **OR** Sugar Cone

■ ■ ■

Fat Free **OR** Damn the Calories

■ ■ ■

Pizza Hut **OR** Domino's

■ ■ ■

Chocolate Milk **OR** Hot Chocolate

■ ■ ■

Tootsie Roll **OR** Tootsie Pop

■ ■ ■

KFC: Regular **OR** Extra-Crispy

Chocolate-Chip Ice Cream **OR**
Chocolate Fudge Ice Cream

∎ ∎ ∎

Prix Fixe Dinner **OR** À la Carte

∎ ∎ ∎

Sweet Pickles **OR** Sour Pickles

∎ ∎ ∎

Salt **OR** Pepper

∎ ∎ ∎

Pistachios **OR** Cashews

∎ ∎ ∎

Ice Cream Soda **OR** Milk Shake

Sushi **OR** *Escargot*

■ ■ ■

Bagel **OR** *English Muffin*

■ ■ ■

Pizza Topping:
Pepperoni **OR** *Mushroom*

■ ■ ■

On Hot Dog: Sauerkraut **OR** *Relish*

■ ■ ■

Peanut Butter **OR** *Jelly*

■ ■ ■

Cook Steak: BBQ **OR** *Oven*

Bourbon **OR** *Scotch*

■ ■ ■

Chalupa **OR** *Burrito*

■ ■ ■

Croutons **OR** *Bacon Bits*

■ ■ ■

Pears: Bosc **OR** *Bartlett*

■ ■ ■

Frozen Food **OR** *Fast Food*

■ ■ ■

Cheddar Cheese **OR** *American Cheese*

■ ■ ■

Meatloaf **OR** *Meatballs*

Ice Cream: Plain **OR** *With Toppings*

■　■　■

Corned Beef **OR** *Pastrami*

■　■　■

Eat Dinner at Bar **OR**
Wait One Hour for Table

■　■　■

Restaurant Seating: Booth **OR** *Table*

■　■　■

Espresso **OR** *Cappuccino*

■　■　■

Sandwich: Open Face **OR** *Closed Face*

Lettuce: Romaine **OR** *Iceberg*

■ ■ ■

Steak Fries **OR** *Curly Fries*

■ ■ ■

Cantaloupe **OR** *Honeydew*

■ ■ ■

Doughnuts: Chocolate **OR** *Jelly-Filled*

■ ■ ■

Sugar Daddy **OR** *Sugar Babies*

■ ■ ■

Apple Juice **OR** *Cranberry Juice*

■ ■ ■

Dinner: Buffet **OR** *Sit Down*

Jenny Craig **OR** Weight Watchers

■ ■ ■

Cookie Dough: Raw **OR** Baked

■ ■ ■

Lamb Chop **OR** Veal Chop

■ ■ ■

Manhattan Clam Chowder **OR**
New England Clam Chowder

■ ■ ■

Frogs' Legs: Delicacy **OR** Gross

■ ■ ■

Brisket **OR** Roast Beef

Licorice: Red **OR** *Black*

▪ ▪ ▪

Black Tea **OR** *Herbal Tea*

▪ ▪ ▪

Szechuan **OR** *Mandarin*

▪ ▪ ▪

Hospital Food **OR** *Airline Food*

▪ ▪ ▪

Lollipop: Lick **OR** *Chew*

▪ ▪ ▪

Rye Bread **OR** *Pumpernickel*

Eat Dinner:
Early Bird **OR** *Midnight Supper*

■ ■ ■

Eat Lunch: 11:00 A.M. **OR** *3:00* P.M.

■ ■ ■

Salsa: Mild **OR** *Hot*

■ ■ ■

Tortilla: Corn **OR** *Flour*

■ ■ ■

Cheeseburger **OR** *Hamburger*

■ ■ ■

Pasta: Angel Hair **OR** *Rigatoni*

Watermelon: With Seeds **OR** *Seedless*

■ ■ ■

Pistachios: Red **OR** *White*

■ ■ ■

Potatoes **OR** *Stuffing*

■ ■ ■

Cauliflower **OR** *Brussels Sprouts*

■ ■ ■

Potato Chips **OR** *Corn Chips*

Baby Care

OR

Kids' Stuff

Breast-Feed **OR** Bottle-Feed

■ ■ ■

Let Kid Cry **OR** Comfort Immediately

■ ■ ■

Big Bird **OR** Barney

■ ■ ■

Child Sleeps in Parents' Bed **OR**
Sleeps in Own Bed

■ ■ ■

Toy Gun:
Child's Play **OR** Not for Youngsters

Live-in Nanny **OR** *Babysitter*

∎ ∎ ∎

Fertility Drugs **OR** *Adoption*

∎ ∎ ∎

Ren **OR** *Stimpy*

∎ ∎ ∎

Preschool **OR** *Learn at Home*

∎ ∎ ∎

Natural Childbirth **OR** *Epidural*

∎ ∎ ∎

Tom **OR** *Jerry*

∎ ∎ ∎

Bozo **OR** *Krusty the Clown*

Learn the Sex of the Unborn Child **OR**
Be Surprised

■ ■ ■

Tweety Bird **OR** *Woodstock*

■ ■ ■

Beavis **OR** *Butt-head*

■ ■ ■

Stay-at-Home Mom **OR** *Career Mom*

■ ■ ■

Yogi Bear **OR** *Boo Boo*

■ ■ ■

Underdog **OR** *Scooby Doo*

Only Child **OR** *One of Several Kids*

■ ■ ■

Old Barbie **OR** *New Barbie*

■ ■ ■

Oscar the Grouch **OR** *Elmo*

■ ■ ■

Rocky **OR** *Bullwinkle*

■ ■ ■

The Flintstones **OR** The Jetsons

■ ■ ■

Rugrats **OR** Doug

■ ■ ■

Comic Book **OR** *Video Game*

Hula Hoop **OR** *Pogo Stick*

■ ■ ■

Slinky **OR** *Yo-yo*

■ ■ ■

Aesop's Fables **OR** *Nursery Rhymes*

■ ■ ■

Candyland **OR** *Chutes and Ladders*

■ ■ ■

Circus **OR** *Carnival*

■ ■ ■

Roller Coaster **OR** *Bumper Cars*

■ ■ ■

Beanie Babies **OR** *Pokémon*

Drop 'Em Off at the Mall **OR**
Parent Chaperon

■ ■ ■

Clothing Styles:
Parents Select **OR** *Kids Select*

■ ■ ■

Infant: Snugli **OR** *Strollers*

■ ■ ■

Jacks **OR** *Marbles*

■ ■ ■

Mickey Mouse **OR** *Donald Duck*

■ ■ ■

Little League **OR** *Youth Soccer*

Diapers: Cloth **OR** Disposable

■ ■ ■

Harry Potter **OR** The Magic Schoolbus

■ ■ ■

Medicine: Liquid **OR** Chewable

■ ■ ■

Kiddy Ride: Piggyback **OR** Horsie

■ ■ ■

Dodge Ball **OR** Kick Ball

■ ■ ■

Day Camp **OR** Sleep-Away Camp

■ ■ ■

See-Saw **OR** Monkey Bars

Legos **OR** *Lincoln Logs*

■ ■ ■

Pacifier **OR** *Thumb*

■ ■ ■

Simon Says **OR** *Duck, Duck, Goose*

■ ■ ■

Merry-Go-Round **OR** *Ferris Wheel*

■ ■ ■

Fun House **OR** *Haunted House*

■ ■ ■

Kids' Sneakers: Shoelaces **OR** *Velcro*

Zoo **OR** *Aquarium*

■ ■ ■

Hide **OR** *Seek*

■ ■ ■

Play-Doh **OR** *Silly Putty*

■ ■ ■

Do Homework:
Before Dinner **OR** *After Dinner*

■ ■ ■

Bert **OR** *Ernie*

■ ■ ■

Snowball Fight **OR** *Pillow Fight*

Baby Food: Homemade **OR** *Jarred*

■ ■ ■

Baby Gap **OR** *Gymboree*

■ ■ ■

Balmex **OR** *Desitin*

■ ■ ■

Gumby **OR** *Pokey*

■ ■ ■

Spanking Children:
Appropriate **OR** *Cruel*

■ ■ ■

Bugs Bunny **OR** *Daffy Duck*

Corporal Punishment in School:
Old-Fashioned **OR** *Still Effective*

∎ ∎ ∎

Dwarf: Sneezy **OR** *Grumpy*

∎ ∎ ∎

Break Mom's Vase: Fess Up **OR** *Cover Up*

∎ ∎ ∎

Coyote **OR** *Roadrunner*

∎ ∎ ∎

Cowboys **OR** *Indians*

∎ ∎ ∎

Cops **OR** *Robbers*

Howdy Doody **OR** *Lambchop*

■ ■ ■

Playpen **OR** *Roam Free*

■ ■ ■

Sesame Street **OR** Teletubbies

■ ■ ■

Etch-A-Sketch **OR** *Blocks*

■ ■ ■

Rubik's Cube: Cool **OR** *Geeky*

■ ■ ■

Twins: Identical **OR** *Fraternal*

Finger-Paint **OR** *Paint by Numbers*

■ ■ ■

Limbo **OR** *Twister*

■ ■ ■

Sega Dreamcast **OR** *Sony PlayStation*

■ ■ ■

Parenting: Tough **OR** *Tender*

■ ■ ■

Candy Cigarettes: Harmless **OR** *Harmful*

■ ■ ■

Sleepover **OR** *Play Date*

Same-Sex Parents Adopt Child:

Problematic **OR** *No Problem*

■ ■ ■

Comic Book: X-men **OR** Spawn

■ ■ ■

Baseball Cards:

Collect for Fun **OR** *Investment*

■ ■ ■

Water-Balloon Fight **OR** *Slip 'n' Slide*

People

OR

Celebrities

Laurel **OR** *Hardy*

■ ■ ■

Martin **OR** *Lewis*

■ ■ ■

Abbott **OR** *Costello*

■ ■ ■

Sonny **OR** *Cher*

■ ■ ■

The Fonz **OR** *Vinnie Barbarino*

■ ■ ■

David Letterman **OR** *Jay Leno*

■ ■ ■

Oprah Winfrey **OR** *Rosie O'Donnell*

Galloping Gourmet **OR** *Julia Child*

■ ■ ■

Daniel Boone **OR** *Davy Crockett*

■ ■ ■

Twiggy **OR** *Kate Moss*

■ ■ ■

Bach **OR** *Beethoven*

■ ■ ■

Dracula **OR** *Frankenstein*

■ ■ ■

John Grisham **OR** *Stephen King*

■ ■ ■

Robert Redford **OR** *Brad Pitt*

Ann Landers **OR** Dear Abby

∎ ∎ ∎

Felix **OR** Oscar

∎ ∎ ∎

Kramer **OR** George

∎ ∎ ∎

Siskel **OR** Ebert

∎ ∎ ∎

Ralph Kramden **OR** Ed Norton

∎ ∎ ∎

John Belushi **OR** Chris Farley

∎ ∎ ∎

Howard Stern **OR** Don Imus

David Copperfield **OR** *Harry Houdini*

■ ■ ■

Simon **OR** *Garfunkel*

■ ■ ■

Mariah Carey **OR** *Whitney Houston*

■ ■ ■

Robin Williams **OR** *Billy Crystal*

■ ■ ■

Melanie Griffith **OR** *Don Johnson*

■ ■ ■

Laverne **OR** *Shirley*

■ ■ ■

Dustin Hoffman **OR** *Robert De Niro*

Jack Lemmon **OR** Walter Matthau

∎ ∎ ∎

Fred Astaire **OR** Ginger Rogers

∎ ∎ ∎

Clark Gable **OR** Cary Grant

∎ ∎ ∎

Tony Bennett **OR** Harry Connick, Jr.

∎ ∎ ∎

O. J. Simpson: Bum Rap **OR** Bum

∎ ∎ ∎

John Glenn **OR** Neil Armstrong

∎ ∎ ∎

Johnny Cochran **OR** Marcia Clark

Fran Drescher **OR** *Lucille Ball*

■ ■ ■

Regis Philbin **OR** *Kathie Lee Gifford*

■ ■ ■

Lone Ranger **OR** *Tonto*

■ ■ ■

Alec Baldwin **OR** *Kim Basinger*

■ ■ ■

Irving Berlin's Legacy: "White Christmas"
OR *"God Bless America"*

■ ■ ■

Bruce Willis **OR** *Demi Moore*

Johnny Carson **OR** *Ed McMahon*

■ ■ ■

Frankie Avalon **OR** *Annette Funnicello*

■ ■ ■

Paula Corbin Jones **OR** *Monica Lewinsky*

■ ■ ■

Cheers: *Kirstie Alley* **OR** *Shelley Long*

■ ■ ■

Batman **OR** *Robin*

■ ■ ■

Superman **OR** *Clark Kent*

■ ■ ■

Betty **OR** *Veronica*

Wally **OR** *The Beaver*

. . .

Madonna **OR** *Roseanne*

. . .

Darrin of Bewitched:
Dick York **OR** *Dick Sargent*

. . .

Alfalfa **OR** *Spanky*

. . .

Richard Burton **OR** *Elizabeth Taylor*

. . .

Adam **OR** *Eve*

Spike Lee **OR** *Ken Burns*

■ ■ ■

Rowan **OR** *Martin*

■ ■ ■

Thelma **OR** *Louise*

■ ■ ■

Jason **OR** *Freddie Krueger*

■ ■ ■

Humphrey Bogart **OR** *Lauren Bacall*

■ ■ ■

Yoko Ono:
Broke Up the Beatles **OR** *Innocent Bystander*

Cheech **OR** *Chong*

■ ■ ■

Las Vegas Entertainer:
Elvis Presley **OR** *Wayne Newton*

■ ■ ■

Hank Williams **OR** *Hank Williams, Jr.*

■ ■ ■

Mick Jagger **OR** *Keith Richards*

■ ■ ■

Paul Reubens **OR** *Pee Wee Herman*

■ ■ ■

Christopher Reeve's Legacy:
Superman **OR** *Advocate for the Disabled*

Romeo **OR** *Juliet*

■ ■ ■

Joan Rivers **OR** *Phyllis Diller*

■ ■ ■

Pamela Anderson **OR** *Tommy Lee*

■ ■ ■

Goober **OR** *Gomer Pyle*

■ ■ ■

Charles Lindbergh **OR** *Amelia Earhart*

■ ■ ■

Nicolas Cage's Best "Vegas" Movie:
Leaving Las **OR** Honeymoon In

Paul McCartney **OR** John Lennon

■ ■ ■

Milton Berle **OR** Jack Benny

■ ■ ■

The Joker **OR** The Riddler

■ ■ ■

Kelsey Grammer **OR** Frasier Crane

■ ■ ■

Lead Singer of Genesis:
Peter Gabriel **OR** Phil Collins

■ ■ ■

M*A*S*H: Colonel Henry Blake **OR**
Colonel Sherman T. Potter

Less Believable David Hasselhoff TV Show:

Knight Rider **OR** Baywatch

■ ■ ■

Don Rickles **OR** *Andrew "Dice" Clay*

■ ■ ■

Jesse "the Body" Ventura's Legacy:

Wrestler **OR** Governor

■ ■ ■

Mia Farrow **OR** *Soon-Yi*

■ ■ ■

Linda Tripp **OR** *Brutus*

■ ■ ■

George Burns **OR** *Gracie Allen*

Marla Maples **OR** *Ivana Trump*

■ ■ ■

Dharma **OR** *Greg*

■ ■ ■

Gilda Radner **OR** *Jane Curtin*

■ ■ ■

Joey Buttafuoco **OR** *Amy Fisher*

■ ■ ■

Tatum O'Neal **OR** *Kristy McNichol*

■ ■ ■

Richard Pryor **OR** *Chris Rock*

Better Center Hollywood Square:
Paul Lynde **OR** *Whoopi Goldberg*

■ ■ ■

David Hyde Pierce **OR** *Ray Romano*

■ ■ ■

"Who Wants to Marry a Multimillionaire":
Darva Conger **OR** *Rick Rockwell*

■ ■ ■

Better Shaft:
Richard Roundtree **OR** *Samuel L. Jackson*

■ ■ ■

Jennifer Lopez **OR** *Christina Aguilera*

Penn **OR** *Teller*

■ ■ ■

Charlton Heston's Legacy:
Actor **OR** *Gun Advocate*

■ ■ ■

Jean-Claude Van Damme **OR** *Steven Seagal*

■ ■ ■

Bruce Lee **OR** *Jackie Chan*

■ ■ ■

Julia Roberts **OR** *Sandra Bullock*

■ ■ ■

Aretha Franklin **OR** *James Brown*

Jack Kevorkian:

Good Doctor OR Doctors with Fate

■ ■ ■

King Kong OR Godzilla

■ ■ ■

Liza Minnelli OR Judy Garland

■ ■ ■

Shirley MacLain's Legacy:

Actress OR Born Again, Again, Again

■ ■ ■

Dennis Miller's Legacy:

Comedian OR Sportscaster

Entertainment

OR

Media

Sound of Music **OR**

The Wizard of Oz

■ ■ ■

Star Wars **OR**

The Phantom Menace

■ ■ ■

Rolling Stones **OR** *The Beatles*

■ ■ ■

Scrabble **OR** *Monopoly*

■ ■ ■

Blackjack **OR** *Craps*

■ ■ ■

Movie Rental **OR** *Movie Theater*

Opera **OR** *Ballet*

■ ■ ■

Rap Music **OR** *Punk Rock*

■ ■ ■

Doonesbury **OR** Garfield

■ ■ ■

ER **OR** Chicago Hope

■ ■ ■

Art: Impressionist **OR** *Abstract*

■ ■ ■

Dateline **OR** 60 Minutes

Sports Illustrated **OR**
Popular Mechanics

■   ■   ■

Wheel of Fortune **OR** Jeopardy

■   ■   ■

Les Misérables **OR**
Phantom of the Opera

■   ■   ■

Glamour **OR** Cosmopolitan

■   ■   ■

Checkers **OR** *Chess*

■   ■   ■

Fiction **OR** *Nonfiction*

Piano **OR** *Drums*

■ ■ ■

Playboy **OR** Penthouse

■ ■ ■

AM **OR** *FM*

■ ■ ■

Listen to Radio **OR** *Play Your Own Music*

■ ■ ■

Time **OR** Newsweek

■ ■ ■

Twist **OR** *Hustle*

■ ■ ■

Park **OR** *Museum*

Potato-Sack Race **OR** Three-Legged Race

■ ■ ■

Big-Screen TV **OR** Watchman

■ ■ ■

Days of Our Lives **OR**
General Hospital

■ ■ ■

Tap-dancing **OR** Ballroom Dancing

■ ■ ■

Theater: Broadway **OR** Community

■ ■ ■

Musical **OR** Drama

Odd Couple: *Movie* OR *TV Show*

■ ■ ■

Improvisation: Quick-Witted OR *Nitwitted*

■ ■ ■

Grateful Dead:
Rock On OR *Too Old to Rock*

■ ■ ■

The Andy Griffith Show OR

Beverly Hillbillies

■ ■ ■

Orchestra Seats OR *Mezzanine*

■ ■ ■

Network OR *Cable*

The Simpsons **OR** South Park

■ ■ ■

Hardcover **OR** *Paperback*

■ ■ ■

VH1 **OR** *MTV*

■ ■ ■

Gin Rummy **OR** *Poker*

■ ■ ■

Monopoly Token: Race Car **OR** *Doggie*

■ ■ ■

Direct a Blockbuster Movie **OR**
Pen a Best-Seller

It's a Wonderful Life **OR**

Miracle on Thirty-Fourth Street

■ ■ ■

Beverly Hills 90210 **OR** Melrose Place

■ ■ ■

Piano: Steinway **OR** *Yamaha*

■ ■ ■

Daytime TV:
Soap Opera **OR** *Game Show*

■ ■ ■

Claymation **OR** *Animation*

■ ■ ■

Whale Watching **OR** *Swim with the Dolphins*

Jurassic Park: *The Movie* OR *The Book*

. . .

Square Dancing OR *Line Dancing*

. . .

Organ Music: Ballpark OR *Church*

. . .

Romance Novel OR *Detective Novel*

. . .

Nine Inch Nails OR *Smashing Pumpkins*

. . .

Public Library OR *Bookstore*

. . .

Hokey Pokey OR *Alley Cat*

Itzhak Perlman on the Violin **OR**

Vladimir Horowitz on the Piano

■ ■ ■

Partridge Family **OR**

Brady Bunch

■ ■ ■

National Enquirer **OR** People

■ ■ ■

Salt-N-Pepa **OR** *Spice Girls*

■ ■ ■

Golden Girls **OR** Sunshine Boys

■ ■ ■

Black Crowes **OR** *Counting Crows*

Citizen Kane **OR**

Gone with the Wind

■ ■ ■

Sonnet **OR** *Limerick*

■ ■ ■

Michelangelo's "David" **OR**

Rodin's *"The Thinker"*

■ ■ ■

Rat Pack **OR** *Brat Pack*

■ ■ ■

Double Feature **OR** *Doubleheader*

Foosball **OR** *Pinball*

■ ■ ■

"Mona Lisa" **OR** *"Whistler's Mother"*

■ ■ ■

Roulette: Red **OR** *Black*

■ ■ ■

Entertainment Tonight **OR**

Access Hollywood

■ ■ ■

Yahtzee **OR** *Jenga*

■ ■ ■

The Monkees **OR** *Spinal Tap*

Horseback Ride **OR** *Nature Walk*

■ ■ ■

Metallica **OR** *Mötley Crüe*

■ ■ ■

Poker: Five-Card Stud **OR** *Draw*

■ ■ ■

HBO **OR** *Showtime*

■ ■ ■

La Bohème **OR** Carmen

■ ■ ■

Baritone **OR** *Tenor*

The Dating Game **OR**
The Newlywed Game

■ ■ ■

Trumpet **OR** *Trombone*

■ ■ ■

Flashdance **OR** Footloose

■ ■ ■

Dilbert **OR** Ziggy

■ ■ ■

Casablanca **OR** On the Waterfront

■ ■ ■

The Graduate **OR** Rain Man

Do Crossword Puzzle in: Ink **OR** *Pencil*

■　■　■

Music: Heavy Metal **OR** *Classical*

■　■　■

Movie: X-Rated **OR** *G-Rated*

■　■　■

Lottery Winners:
Lump Sum **OR** *Weekly Annuity*

■　■　■

Backstreet Boys **OR** *Beach Boys*

■　■　■

Board Game **OR** *Computer Game*

Bad Movie in Theater: Leave **OR** *Stay*

■ ■ ■

Charlie's Angels **OR** *Hell's Angels*

■ ■ ■

Jazz **OR** *Blues*

■ ■ ■

Mime: Art Form **OR** *Silent Killer*

■ ■ ■

Charades **OR** *Pictionary*

■ ■ ■

Costume Party **OR** *Surprise Party*

Better Budweiser Spokesmen:
Lizards OR *"What's Up" Guys*

. . .

News Source: Newspapers OR *Television*

. . .

Ventriloquist OR *Impressionist*

. . .

Who Wants to Be a Millionaire OR
Who Wants to Marry a
Multimillionaire

. . .

VCR OR *DVD*

Fashion

OR

Home Decorating

Zippers **OR** *Buttons*

■　■　■

Shoes: With **OR** *Without Socks*

■　■　■

Peg Leg **OR** *Bell Bottoms*

■　■　■

Miniskirt **OR** *Midi-Skirt*

■　■　■

Furniture: Antiques **OR** *Contemporary*

■　■　■

House **OR** *Apartment*

Suspenders **OR** *Belts*

■ ■ ■

Gloves **OR** *Mittens*

■ ■ ■

Clothing: Solids **OR** *Patterns*

■ ■ ■

Bikini **OR** *One-Piece*

■ ■ ■

Toupee **OR** *Hair Weave*

■ ■ ■

Architecture: Gothic **OR** *Roman*

■ ■ ■

Gray **OR** *Bald*

Earrings: Clip-On **OR** *Pierced*

■ ■ ■

Tattoos **OR** *Piercings*

■ ■ ■

Tissue **OR** *Handkerchief*

■ ■ ■

Button-Down **OR** *Pullover*

■ ■ ■

Necklace **OR** *Bracelet*

■ ■ ■

Cowboy Hat **OR** *Baseball Cap*

■ ■ ■

Satin **OR** *Silk*

Headband **OR** *Scrunchie*

■ ■ ■

Umbrella **OR** *Raincoat*

■ ■ ■

Five O'Clock Shadow **OR** *Clean-Shaven*

■ ■ ■

Beard **OR** *Mustache*

■ ■ ■

Home Architecture: Ranch **OR** *Colonial*

■ ■ ■

Bunk Bed **OR** *Waterbed*

■ ■ ■

Double-Breasted **OR** *Single-Breasted*

Kmart **OR** *Saks*

■ ■ ■

Perm **OR** *Crew Cut*

■ ■ ■

Sunblock **OR** *Suntan*

■ ■ ■

Put on Sweater **OR** *Turn Up Heat*

■ ■ ■

Pack Clothes **OR** *Unpack Clothes*

■ ■ ■

Place Mat **OR** *Tablecloth*

■ ■ ■

Queen-size Bed **OR** *King-size Bed*

Make Bed **OR** *Leave Unmade*

■ ■ ■

Dress Left **OR** *Dress Right*

■ ■ ■

Socks in Drawer: Roll **OR** *Fold*

■ ■ ■

Underwear: White **OR** *Color*

■ ■ ■

Cosmetic Surgery **OR**
Let Nature Take Its Course

■ ■ ■

Basement **OR** *Attic*

Cotton **OR** Polyester

■ ■ ■

Coin Purse **OR** Loose Change in Pockets

■ ■ ■

Remodel **OR** Move

■ ■ ■

Bunk Bed: Top **OR** Bottom

■ ■ ■

Reebok **OR** Nike

■ ■ ■

Body Piercing: Nose **OR** Belly Button

■ ■ ■

Carpeting **OR** Wood Floors

Mattress: Soft **OR** *Firm*

■ ■ ■

Recessed Lighting **OR** *Lamps*

■ ■ ■

Fine Antiques **OR** *Collectibles*

■ ■ ■

Cubic Zirconia **OR** *Real Diamonds*

■ ■ ■

Condo **OR** *Co-Op*

■ ■ ■

Backyard: Swimming Pool **OR** *Tennis Court*

■ ■ ■

Manicure **OR** *Pedicure*

Leisure Suit **OR** Nehru Jacket

■ ■ ■

Eyebrows: Tweeze **OR** Wax

■ ■ ■

Lipstick: Glossy **OR** Matte Finish

■ ■ ■

Hangers: Wire **OR** Wooden

■ ■ ■

Christmas Tree: Artificial **OR** Live

■ ■ ■

Tabletop: Glass **OR** Wood

■ ■ ■

Chair: Rocker **OR** Recliner

Landlord **OR** *Tenant*

■ ■ ■

Eyeglasses **OR** *Contact Lenses*

■ ■ ■

Chapped Lips: Chapstick **OR** *Lick Lips*

■ ■ ■

Grandfather Clock **OR** *Cuckoo Clock*

■ ■ ■

Docksiders **OR** *Hush Puppies*

■ ■ ■

Business Suit: Pinstripe **OR** *Solid*

■ ■ ■

Mood Ring **OR** *Love Beads*

Paint **OR** *Wallpaper*

■ ■ ■

Panty Hose: Sheer **OR** *Opaque*

■ ■ ■

Sauna **OR** *Steambath*

■ ■ ■

Put on First: Sock, Sock, Shoe, Shoe **OR**
Sock, Shoe, Sock, Shoe

■ ■ ■

Wear Underwear Till:
Holes Appear **OR** *Goes Out of Style*

Fur Coat: The Height of Fashion **OR** *The Plight of Fashion*

■ ■ ■

One Size Fits All: Propaganda **OR** *Miracle*

■ ■ ■

Top Sheet of Bed: Tucked in at Foot **OR** *Loose*

■ ■ ■

Curly Hair **OR** *Straight Hair*

■ ■ ■

Color Hair **OR** *Go Gray*

Jeans **OR** *Sweats*

■ ■ ■

Pants **OR** *Shorts*

■ ■ ■

Tuxedo: Rent **OR** *Own*

■ ■ ■

Kitchen **OR** *Bedroom*

■ ■ ■

iving Room **OR** *Dining Room*

■ ■ ■

Mow Lawn Yourself **OR** *Hire Gardener*

Sideburns: Long **OR** *Short*

∎ ∎ ∎

Bulb: Incandescent **OR** *Halogen*

∎ ∎ ∎

Pine **OR** *Mahogany*

∎ ∎ ∎

Paper Cups **OR** *Fine Glassware*

∎ ∎ ∎

Man's Dress Shirt: Starch **OR** *No Starch*

∎ ∎ ∎

Hemlines:
Above the Knee **OR** *Below the Knee*

Jewelry: Gold **OR** *Silver*

■ ■ ■

Guy's Bathing Suit:
Speedos **OR** *Swim Trunks*

■ ■ ■

Dye Hair Blonde: Cool **OR** *Fool*

■ ■ ■

Tie-Dye **OR** *Suit and Tie*

■ ■ ■

House: Two-Story **OR** *One-Story*

■ ■ ■

Flats **OR** *Heels*

Home Security: Dog **OR** Alarm

■ ■ ■

Diving Board **OR** Water Slide

■ ■ ■

Wear Baseball Cap:
Forward **OR** Backward

■ ■ ■

Boots **OR** Rubbers

■ ■ ■

Preferred Servant: Butler **OR** Maid

Technology

OR

Finance

Cell Phones in Movie Theaters:
Turn On OR Turn Off

■ ■ ■

IBM OR Apple

■ ■ ■

Satellite Dish OR Cable TV

■ ■ ■

NASDAQ OR NYSE

■ ■ ■

Beta OR VHS

■ ■ ■

Matches OR Cigarette Lighter

Bull **OR** *Bear*

■ ■ ■

Telephone: Push-Button **OR** *Rotary*

■ ■ ■

Candles **OR** *Flashlight*

■ ■ ■

Knife **OR** *Electric Carver*

■ ■ ■

Inkjet **OR** *Laser Jet*

■ ■ ■

Checking Account **OR** *Money Market*

■ ■ ■

Computer Banking **OR** *Write Checks*

Answering Machine **OR** *Voice Mail*

■ ■ ■

Snow Shovel **OR** *Snow Blower*

■ ■ ■

Root Canal **OR** *Pull the Tooth*

■ ■ ■

Man **OR** *Machine*

■ ■ ■

U.S. Currency:
New Style Bills **OR** *Old Style Bills*

■ ■ ■

Desktop **OR** *Laptop*

Microwave **OR** *Convection Oven*

■   ■   ■

Stocks **OR** *Bonds*

■   ■   ■

Letter Opener **OR** *Finger*

■   ■   ■

Type **OR** *Longhand*

■   ■   ■

ATM **OR** *Teller*

■   ■   ■

Turbo Tax **OR** *Accountant*

■   ■   ■

Call Waiting **OR** *Caller ID*

Whole Life Insurance OR
Term Life Insurance

■ ■ ■

Tax Audit OR *Rectal Exam*

■ ■ ■

Digital Watch OR *Clock Face*

■ ■ ■

Mortgage:
Adjustable Rate OR *Fixed Rate*

■ ■ ■

Low Inflation OR *Low Unemployment*

Barron's **OR** Wall Street Journal

■ ■ ■

Laser Eye Surgery **OR** *Corrective Lenses*

■ ■ ■

Electric Blanket **OR** *Turn Up the Heat*

■ ■ ■

IRA: Traditional **OR** *Roth*

■ ■ ■

Company: Private **OR** *Publicly Held*

■ ■ ■

Automatic Sprinkler **OR**
Water Lawn Yourself

Investment:

Real Estate **OR** *Commodities*

■ ■ ■

Treasury Bonds **OR** *U.S. Savings Bonds*

■ ■ ■

Industrial Revolution **OR** *Internet Revolution*

■ ■ ■

Buy **OR** *Sell*

■ ■ ■

Blue Chips **OR** *Penny Stocks*

■ ■ ■

Borrow Money from Relatives **OR** *Receive Government Stipend*

Mutual Funds: No Load **OR** *Load*

■ ■ ■

Stocks: A Shares **OR** *B Shares*

■ ■ ■

Dow Jones **OR** *Standard & Poors*

■ ■ ■

Microsoft: Trendsetter **OR** *Monopoly*

■ ■ ■

E-mail **OR** *Telephone Call*

■ ■ ■

Fax **OR** *Overnight FedEx*

Keep Family Budget OR *Wing It*

■ ■ ■

Portfolio Strategy:
Conservative OR *Aggressive*

■ ■ ■

Given Excessive Change:
Return to Cashier OR *Pocket It*

■ ■ ■

10-Year-Old's Weekly Allowance:
$1 OR *$10*

■ ■ ■

Homeless Person Asks for 25 Cents:
Give OR *Ignore*

Bankruptcy: Chance to Start Again **OR**
Coward's Way Out

■ ■ ■

Friend Asks for Loan:
Bad Idea **OR** *Good Idea*

■ ■ ■

Dell **OR** *Gateway*

■ ■ ■

American Express **OR** *Visa*

■ ■ ■

Bill Gates **OR** *Jeff Bezos*

■ ■ ■

Invest $10,000: Amazon.com **OR** *Yahoo*

Thomas Alva Edison **OR**
Alexander Graham Bell

■ ■ ■

Greater Service to Mankind:
Airplane **OR** *Computer*

■ ■ ■

Copernicus **OR** *Galileo*

■ ■ ■

Mid-Cap **OR** *Small-Cap*

■ ■ ■

Greater Invention:
Microwave **OR** *Birth-Control Pills*

Computer Chat Rooms: Fun **OR** *Dangerous*

∎ ∎ ∎

eToys **OR** *Toys "R" Us*

∎ ∎ ∎

Bug Zapper **OR** *Citronella*

∎ ∎ ∎

Coupons: Save Cents **OR** *Waste of Time*

∎ ∎ ∎

Cloud Seeding: Drought Prevention **OR**
Don't Mess with Mother Nature

∎ ∎ ∎

Binoculars **OR** *Microscope*

10-Year Treasury Note **OR**
30-Year Treasury Note

■ ■ ■

Mortgage: 30 Years **OR** *15 Years*

■ ■ ■

Commodities: Pork Bellies **OR** *Coffee*

■ ■ ■

Social Security Benefits:
Age 65 **OR** *Age 67*

■ ■ ■

Credit Card **OR** *Debit Card*

Stock Transaction:

Broker **OR** *On-line Trade*

■ ■ ■

Lights: Dimmer **OR** *Switch*

■ ■ ■

Save: Time **OR** *Money*

■ ■ ■

Save for Retirement via:

Stock Market **OR** *CD*

Name Game

OR

Rhyme Time

Mary Tyler Moore **OR** *Mary Poppins*

■ ■ ■

Dudley Do-Right **OR** *Dudley Moore*

■ ■ ■

Miss America **OR** *Miss Piggy*

■ ■ ■

Jackie Gleason **OR** *Jackie Robinson*

■ ■ ■

Dr. Ruth **OR** *Dr. Seuss*

■ ■ ■

Goldielocks **OR** *Goldie Hawn*

Tom Cruise **OR** *Tom Hanks*

∎ ∎ ∎

Woody Allen **OR** *Woody Harrelson*

∎ ∎ ∎

Queen Latifah **OR** *Queen Elizabeth*

∎ ∎ ∎

Cindy Crawford **OR** *Cindy Brady*

∎ ∎ ∎

Carol Burnett **OR** *Carroll O'Connor*

∎ ∎ ∎

Dalai Lama **OR** *Dolly Parton*

∎ ∎ ∎

Ronald McDonald **OR** *Ronald Reagan*

Mr. Magoo **OR** Mr. T

■ ■ ■

Kevin Costner **OR** Kevin Kline

■ ■ ■

Henry Kissinger **OR** Henry Aaron

■ ■ ■

Frank Sinatra **OR** Frank Gifford

■ ■ ■

Reggie Jackson **OR** Michael Jackson

■ ■ ■

Buck Rogers **OR** Mr. Rogers

■ ■ ■

Mother Goose **OR** Mother Nature

Paul Newman **OR** *Newman!* (Seinfeld)

■ ■ ■

John Denver **OR** *Bob Denver*

■ ■ ■

Captain Kirk **OR** *Captain Picard*

■ ■ ■

Tina Turner **OR** *Ted Turner*

■ ■ ■

Michael Douglas **OR** *Kirk Douglas*

■ ■ ■

William Shakespeare **OR** *William Hurt*

■ ■ ■

Rob Reiner **OR** *Carl Reiner*

Jimmy Stewart **OR** *Martha Stewart*

■ ■ ■

Harrison Ford **OR** *Gerald Ford*

■ ■ ■

Dr. Spock **OR** *Mr. Spock*

■ ■ ■

Ted Danson **OR** *Ted Koppel*

■ ■ ■

Audrey Hepburn **OR** *Katharine Hepburn*

■ ■ ■

Dick Tracy **OR** *Spencer Tracy*

■ ■ ■

Energizer Bunny **OR** *Easter Bunny*

Christie Brinkley **OR** David Brinkley

• • •

Burt Lancaster **OR** Burt Reynolds

• • •

Bill Murray **OR** Bill Cosby

• • •

Matt Dillon **OR** Matt Damon

• • •

Gene Kelly **OR** Grace Kelly

• • •

Larry King **OR** Don King

Arnold Schwarzenegger **OR** *Arnold Palmer*

■ ■ ■

Donny Osmond **OR** *Marie Osmond*

■ ■ ■

Shania Twain **OR** *Mark Twain*

■ ■ ■

Richard Simmons **OR** *Gene Simmons*

■ ■ ■

Tony Curtis **OR** *Jamie Lee Curtis*

■ ■ ■

Billy Joel **OR** *Billie Jean King*

Natalie Cole **OR** Nat King Cole

∎ ∎ ∎

Barbra Streisand **OR** Barbara Walters

∎ ∎ ∎

Bob Hope **OR** Bob Dylan

∎ ∎ ∎

Andie McDowell **OR** Andy Rooney

∎ ∎ ∎

Shaquille O'Neal **OR** Ryan O'Neal

∎ ∎ ∎

Meg Ryan **OR** Meg Tilly

∎ ∎ ∎

James Monroe **OR** Marilyn Monroe

Jerry Stiller **OR** *Ben Stiller*

■ ■ ■

Richard Dreyfuss **OR** *Julia Louis-Dreyfuss*

■ ■ ■

Drew Barrymore **OR** *Drew Carey*

■ ■ ■

Mel Gibson **OR** *Mel Brooks*

■ ■ ■

Charles Darwin **OR** *Charles Dickens*

■ ■ ■

Ernest Hemingway **OR** *Mariel Hemingway*

Anthony Edwards **OR** *Anthony Hopkins*

. . .

Jim Morrison **OR** *Jim Carrey*

. . .

Florence Nightingale **OR** *Florence Henderson*

. . .

Winona Ryder **OR** *Wynonna Judd*

. . .

Courtney Cox **OR** *Courtney Love*

. . .

Tiny Tim (Dickens) **OR**
Tiny Tim ("Tiptoe Through the Tulips")

Marilyn Manson **OR** Marilyn Chambers

■ ■ ■

Barney Fife **OR** Barney Rubble

■ ■ ■

Joan Van Ark **OR** Joan of Arc

■ ■ ■

John Goodman **OR** Benny Goodman

■ ■ ■

Smokey Robinson **OR** Smokey the Bear

■ ■ ■

Ulysses S. Grant **OR** Amy Grant

■ ■ ■

Vanna White **OR** Betty White

Harry Belafonte **OR** Shari Belafonte

■ ■ ■

Shirley Temple **OR** Shirley Jones

■ ■ ■

Ally McBeal **OR** Ali McGraw

■ ■ ■

Tom Jones **OR** Indiana Jones

■ ■ ■

Arthur Schechter **OR** Paula Schechter

■ ■ ■

Mae West **OR** Adam West

■ ■ ■

Walt Whitman **OR** Walt Disney

Marv Albert **OR** *Fat Albert*

■ ■ ■

Larry Holmes **OR** *Sherlock Holmes*

■ ■ ■

Jerry Springer **OR** *Jerry Falwell*

■ ■ ■

Charlie Sheen **OR** *Martin Sheen*

■ ■ ■

Heidi Fleiss **OR** *Heidi*

■ ■ ■

Halle Berry **OR** *Chuck Berry*

■ ■ ■

Eliza Dolittle **OR** *Dr. Dolittle*

Ozzie Nelson **OR** *Ozzie Osborne*

■ ■ ■

Red Foxx **OR** *Michael J. Fox*

■ ■ ■

Jonathan Winters **OR** *Shelly Winters*

■ ■ ■

Leonardo da Vinci **OR** *Leonardo DiCaprio*

■ ■ ■

Dan Rather **OR** *Dan Aykroyd*

■ ■ ■

Little Richard **OR** *Little Red Riding Hood*

■ ■ ■

Sean Penn **OR** *Pig Pen*

James Dean **OR** James Bond

■ ■ ■

Diana Ross **OR** Betsy Ross

■ ■ ■

Tug McGraw **OR** Tim McGraw

■ ■ ■

Paul Reiser **OR** Paul Shaffer

■ ■ ■

F. Scott Fitzgerald **OR** F. Lee Bailey

■ ■ ■

Geena Davis **OR** Terrell Davis

■ ■ ■

Lauryn Hill **OR** Faith Hill

James Cagney **OR** *James Woods*

■ ■ ■

Will Rogers **OR** *Will Smith*

■ ■ ■

Jim Bakker **OR** *Tammy Faye Bakker*

■ ■ ■

Tim Duncan **OR** *Sandy Duncan*

■ ■ ■

Natalie Wood **OR** *Natalie Merchant*

■ ■ ■

Ahmad Rashad **OR** *Phylicia Rashad*

■ ■ ■

Michelle Phillips **OR** *MacKenzie Phillips*

Bart Starr **OR** *Bart Simpson*

■　■　■

Mary Lou Retton **OR** *Marilu Henner*

■　■　■

Conan O'Brien **OR** *Conan the Barbarian*

■　■　■

Albert Einstein **OR** *Albert Brooks*

■　■　■

John Wayne **OR** *Bruce Wayne*

■　■　■

Peter Sellers **OR** *Peter Lawford*

■　■　■

Alice Cooper **OR** *Alice in Wonderland*

Glen Campbell **OR** *Naomi Campbell*

∎   ∎   ∎

Morgan Freeman **OR** *Morgan Fairchild*

∎   ∎   ∎

Eric Clapton **OR** *Eric Dickerson*

∎   ∎   ∎

Duke Ellington **OR** *Duke Snider*

∎   ∎   ∎

Amy Irving **OR** *Julius Erving*

∎   ∎   ∎

Noah Wyle **OR** *Noah*

The World

OR

Landmarks

Retirement Home: Arizona **OR** *Florida*

■ ■ ■

London **OR** *Paris*

■ ■ ■

Landlocked **OR** *Coastal*

■ ■ ■

River **OR** *Lake*

■ ■ ■

Mountain **OR** *Valley*

■ ■ ■

Palm Tree **OR** *Pine Tree*

North Dakota **OR** *South Dakota*

■ ■ ■

Sodom **OR** *Gomorra*

■ ■ ■

Mars **OR** *Venus*

■ ■ ■

City **OR** *Suburbs*

■ ■ ■

Aspen **OR** *Vail*

■ ■ ■

Golden Gate Bridge **OR**
The English Channel

Bridge **OR** Tunnel

■ ■ ■

Hurricanes **OR** Tornadoes

■ ■ ■

High-Pressure System **OR**
Low-Pressure System

■ ■ ■

Australia **OR** New Zealand

■ ■ ■

Black Sea **OR** Red Sea

■ ■ ■

Lake Erie **OR** Lake Michigan

East **OR** *West*

■ ■ ■

Niagara Falls **OR** *Mississippi River*

■ ■ ■

North **OR** *South*

■ ■ ■

Iran **OR** *Iraq*

■ ■ ■

Red Square **OR** *Times Square*

■ ■ ■

Pool **OR** *Beach*

■ ■ ■

The Sphinx **OR** *The Pyramids*

Washington Monument OR

Lincoln Memorial

■ ■ ■

Big Dipper OR *Milky Way*

■ ■ ■

White House OR *U.S. Capitol*

■ ■ ■

Mount Rushmore OR *Stonehenge*

■ ■ ■

Grand Canyon OR *The Redwoods*

■ ■ ■

Mount Everest OR *Mount Sinai*

World Trade Center **OR** Sears Tower

■ ■ ■

Atlantic Ocean **OR** Pacific Ocean

■ ■ ■

North Pole **OR** South Pole

■ ■ ■

Pompeii **OR** Atlantis

■ ■ ■

Las Vegas **OR** Atlantic City

■ ■ ■

Arctic **OR** Antarctica

■ ■ ■

Stalactites **OR** Stalagmites

Desert **OR** *Swamp*

■ ■ ■

New York **OR** *Los Angeles*

■ ■ ■

Rodeo Drive **OR** *Bourbon Street*

■ ■ ■

Global Warming **OR** *Ice Age*

■ ■ ■

Eiffel Tower **OR** *Leaning Tower of Pisa*

■ ■ ■

Cirrus Clouds **OR** *Cumulus Clouds*

■ ■ ■

Lightning **OR** *Thunder*

Sunrise **OR** *Sunset*

■ ■ ■

Longitude **OR** *Latitude*

■ ■ ■

Taj Mahal (Atlantic City) **OR**
Taj Mahal (India)

■ ■ ■

Snow **OR** *Rain*

■ ■ ■

Snow: Winter's Present **OR**
Winter's Cruel Joke

Hawaii OR *Alaska*

■ ■ ■

Urban OR *Rural*

■ ■ ■

UFO's: Real OR *Out of This World*

■ ■ ■

Pluto: Our Solar System's
Ninth Planet OR *Impostor*

■ ■ ■

Life on Mars: Alien Thought OR
Not Out of This World

Disneyland **OR** *Disney World*

∎ ∎ ∎

Mardi Gras **OR** *Le Carnival*

∎ ∎ ∎

Radio City Music Hall **OR**
Carnegie Hall

∎ ∎ ∎

Macy's Thanksgiving Day Parade **OR**
Rose Parade

∎ ∎ ∎

The Smithsonian **OR**
The Museum of Natural History

Dallas's Legacy: Cowboys OR
President Kennedy's Assassination

■ ■ ■

Detroit's Legacy:
Motown OR Automobiles

■ ■ ■

San Antonio's Legacy:
The Alamo OR The Spurs

■ ■ ■

Louvre OR
Metropolitan Museum of Art

Seattle's Legacy:

Grunge Rock **OR** *Space Needle*

■ ■ ■

New Millennium: 2000 **OR** *2001*

■ ■ ■

World War I **OR** *World War II*

■ ■ ■

Hard Rock Cafe **OR** *Planet Hollywood*

■ ■ ■

Canada **OR** *Mexico*

School

OR

Work

Movie Star **OR** Pro Athlete

■ ■ ■

Mortician **OR** Tax Collector

■ ■ ■

Grocer **OR** Farmer

■ ■ ■

Police Officer **OR** Firefighter

■ ■ ■

Doctor **OR** Lawyer

■ ■ ■

Cheerleader **OR** Drum Major

■ ■ ■

Postal Worker **OR** Toll Collector

Taxi Driver **OR** *Taxidermist*

■ ■ ■

Masseuse **OR** *Chiropractor*

■ ■ ■

Briefcase **OR** *Knapsack*

■ ■ ■

Chess Club **OR** *Glee Club*

■ ■ ■

Public School **OR** *Private School*

■ ■ ■

Spiral Notebook **OR** *Loose-Leaf*

■ ■ ■

High School **OR** *Grade School*

Paper Bag **OR** Lunch Box

■   ■   ■

Buy Lunch **OR** Bring Lunch

■   ■   ■

SAT **OR** ACT

■   ■   ■

Study **OR** Cram

■   ■   ■

Basket Weaving 101 **OR** Advanced Calculus

■   ■   ■

State College **OR** Private College

Tuition Paid by Parents **OR**
Work While Attending College

■　■　■

Singer **OR** *Musician*

■　■　■

Judge **OR** *Jury*

■　■　■

Harvard **OR** *Yale*

■　■　■

Bachelor's Degree **OR** *Master's Degree*

■　■　■

Garbage Collector **OR** *Repo Man*

Blue Collar OR *White Collar*

■ ■ ■

Union OR *Nonunion*

■ ■ ■

Parochial School OR *Military School*

■ ■ ■

Army OR *Navy*

■ ■ ■

Gym OR *Lunch*

■ ■ ■

Geometry OR *Algebra*

Hire Headhunter **OR** *Read Classifieds*

■ ■ ■

Work Overtime for:
Comp Time **OR** *Time and a Half*

■ ■ ■

Class President **OR** *Class Clown*

■ ■ ■

Relocate for Promotion **OR** *Stay Put*

■ ■ ■

Career First **OR** *Family First*

Salary:

Discuss with Coworkers OR *Keep Private*

■ ■ ■

Geography OR *History*

■ ■ ■

Graveyard Shift OR *Work Weekends*

■ ■ ■

To Get Expendable Income:
Work After School OR *Rely on Parents*

■ ■ ■

Socialize with Coworkers OR
Keep Friends Separate

Dishonest Coworker:

Tell Boss **OR** *Keep Mouth Shut*

■　■　■

Take Home Work Supplies: Fair **OR** *Unfair*

■　■　■

Shower After Gym Class **OR** *Smell*

■　■　■

Satisfied with a C **OR** *Go for an A*

■　■　■

Cheat on Test **OR** *Fail*

■　■　■

Cliffs Notes **OR** *Read the Book*

Ebonics: Helps Students **OR**
Hinders Students

∎ ∎ ∎

Judge a Beauty Contest **OR**
Photograph an Underwear Shoot

∎ ∎ ∎

DMV Employee: Human **OR** Snail

∎ ∎ ∎

Age 55: Retire **OR** Work

∎ ∎ ∎

Chain Store **OR** Mom and Pop Store

While Working: Whistle **OR** *Hum*

■ ■ ■

Collect Unemployment **OR**
Work for Minimum Wage

■ ■ ■

Brownnose to Advance **OR**
Let Work Speak for Itself

■ ■ ■

Lion Tamer **OR** *Tightrope Walker*

■ ■ ■

Gynecologist **OR** *Plastic Surgeon*

Political Scientist **OR** *Scientist*

■ ■ ■

Athletic Scholarship **OR**
Academic Scholarship

■ ■ ■

Preppie **OR** *Jock*

■ ■ ■

Palm-Top Organizer **OR**
Loose Papers in Wallet

■ ■ ■

Pen: Bic **OR** *Mont Blanc*

Trade School **OR** *College*

■ ■ ■

Trapeze Artist **OR** *Cannonballer*

■ ■ ■

Biology **OR** *Chemistry*

■ ■ ■

English **OR** *Math*

■ ■ ■

Vacation from Job:
Take All at Once **OR** *Break Up*

■ ■ ■

Work Alone **OR** *Work in a Group*

Résumé: Tell the Truth **OR** *Embellish*

■ ■ ■

Coworkers Talking About You in Hallway:
Eavesdrop **OR** *Walk Away*

■ ■ ■

Mental Health Days:
Legit **OR** *Cheating Company*

■ ■ ■

Using Sex Appeal to Advance Career:
Sleazy **OR** *Acceptable*

Boss's Fly Is Open: Tell Him Directly **OR**
E-mail from Coworker's Computer

■   ■   ■

Scabs: Scum **OR**
Whatever It Takes to Earn a Living

■   ■   ■

Test: Multiple Choice **OR** *Essay*

■   ■   ■

Numerical Grades **OR** *Letter Grades*

■   ■   ■

Foreign Language Study:
French **OR** *Spanish*

Summer School OR

Repeat Course Next Year

■ ■ ■

Business Correspondence:

Write a Letter OR *Make Telephone Call*

■ ■ ■

After High School:

Go to College OR *Go to Europe*

■ ■ ■

Astronomy OR *Astrology*

■ ■ ■

Do Weekend's Homework:

Friday Afternoon OR *Sunday Night*

Summer Vacation from College:
Work **OR** *Relax*

■ ■ ■

School Dress Codes: Promote **OR** *Flunk*

■ ■ ■

Shop Class **OR** *Band*

■ ■ ■

After Long Workday: Prepare Dinner
for One Hour **OR** *TV Dinner*

■ ■ ■

First Day of School **OR** *Last Day of School*

■ ■ ■

Eye Doctor **OR** *Dentist*

Employee Fraternization:
Taboo **OR** *Can Do*

■   ■   ■

Accept Layoff **OR** *Dramatic Cut in Pay*

■   ■   ■

High School: Most Likely to Succeed
OR *Most Popular*

Bathroom Babble

OR

Toilet Talk

Set Bathroom Scale:
Above Zero **OR** *Below Zero*

■ ■ ■

Electric Razor **OR** *Razor Blade*

■ ■ ■

Aspirin **OR** *Tylenol*

■ ■ ■

Rectal Thermometer **OR**
Oral Thermometer

■ ■ ■

Homeopathic Medicine **OR**
Prescription Drugs

1 OR # 2

∎ ∎ ∎

Guys: Pee Standing Up OR
Sitting Down

∎ ∎ ∎

Singing in the Shower OR
Singing in the Rain

∎ ∎ ∎

Constipation OR *Diarrhea*

∎ ∎ ∎

Pee in the Shower OR *Hold It In*

∎ ∎ ∎

Noisy Fart OR *Smelly Fart*

Athlete's Foot **OR** *Corn*

■ ■ ■

Pick Your Nose **OR** *Pick Your Nails*

■ ■ ■

Toilet Seat: Up **OR** *Down*

■ ■ ■

Kohler **OR** *Pfister*

■ ■ ■

Scope **OR** *Listerine*

■ ■ ■

Poop **OR** *Get off the Pot*

■ ■ ■

Use Porta-Potty **OR** *Cross Your Legs*

Urinal **OR** *Stall*

■　■　■

Squeeze Toothpaste: Bottom **OR** *Middle*

■　■　■

Toothpaste: Gel **OR** *Paste*

■　■　■

Shave **OR** *Wax*

■　■　■

Comb **OR** *Brush*

■　■　■

Shower in the Morning **OR**
Shower in the Evening

Q-Tip **OR** *Finger*

∎ ∎ ∎

Cut Nails **OR** *Bite Nails*

∎ ∎ ∎

Blow Dry Hair **OR** *Dry Naturally*

∎ ∎ ∎

Liquid Soap **OR** *Bar Soap*

∎ ∎ ∎

Tampons **OR** *Pads*

∎ ∎ ∎

Master Bath: Two Sinks **OR** *One Sink*

∎ ∎ ∎

Potty Train a Baby **OR** *Housebreak a Dog*

Emery Board **OR** *Nail File*

∎ ∎ ∎

Shower Door **OR** *Shower Curtain*

∎ ∎ ∎

In Bath: Bubbles **OR** *Rubber Ducky*

∎ ∎ ∎

Electric Toothbrush **OR** *Regular Toothbrush*

∎ ∎ ∎

Shower Head: Handheld **OR** *Mounted*

∎ ∎ ∎

Antiperspirant **OR** *Deodorant*

∎ ∎ ∎

Cream Rinse **OR** *Conditioner*

Hair Spray **OR** *Mousse*

■ ■ ■

Aftershave **OR** *Cologne*

■ ■ ■

Dental Floss **OR** *Toothpick*

■ ■ ■

Read Book on Toilet **OR** *Contemplate Life*

■ ■ ■

Toilet Paper: White **OR** *Color*

■ ■ ■

Neighbor's Bathroom: Look in Medicine
Cabinet **OR** *Mind Your Business*

Fan **OR** *Air Freshener*

∎ ∎ ∎

If It's Yellow Let It Mellow **OR** *Flush*

∎ ∎ ∎

Wash Hands After Peeing **OR** *Just Zip Up*

∎ ∎ ∎

Stall Out of Toilet Paper:
Borrow **OR** *Improvise*

∎ ∎ ∎

Peeing Men:
Use Underwear Slit **OR** *Go over the Top*

OR
242

Toothpaste **OR** *Baking Soda*

∎ ∎ ∎

Toilet Paper Style: Fold **OR** *Crumple*

∎ ∎ ∎

In Shower, Wash First: Hair **OR** *Body*

∎ ∎ ∎

After Shower, First:
Get Dressed **OR** *Blow Hair*

∎ ∎ ∎

Friend Has Bad Breath:
Tell Him **OR** *Grin and Bear It*

∎ ∎ ∎

Do First in Morning: Shave **OR** *Shower*

Clean Toilet **OR** *Clean Shower*

■ ■ ■

After # 2: Flush, then Zip Up **OR**
Zip Up, then Flush

■ ■ ■

Belch **OR** *Fart*

■ ■ ■

Burp **OR** *Hiccup*

■ ■ ■

In Public with:
Fly Open **OR** *Booger on Nose*

Public Bathroom, Dry Hands with:
Paper Towel **OR** *Air Blower*

■   ■   ■

His and Hers Bath Towels:
Quaint **OR** *Queer*

■   ■   ■

Hot Shower **OR** *Cold Shower*

■   ■   ■

Plumber **OR** *Drano*

■   ■   ■

Brush Teeth:
Side to Side **OR** *Up and Down*

Cars

OR

Transport

Two-Door **OR** Four-Door

■ ■ ■

Foreign Car **OR** Domestic Car

■ ■ ■

Range Rover **OR** Jeep

■ ■ ■

Premium Gas **OR** Regular Gas

■ ■ ■

Car Phone **OR** Cellular Phone

■ ■ ■

Manual Transmission **OR**
Automatic Transmission

Automatic Car Wash **OR** *Wash Car Yourself*

■ ■ ■

Carpool to Work **OR** *Public Transportation*

■ ■ ■

Truck Driver **OR** *Bus Driver*

■ ■ ■

Valet Park **OR** *Self-Park*

■ ■ ■

Right Lane **OR** *Left Lane*

■ ■ ■

Yellow Light: Stop **OR** *Speed Up*

■ ■ ■

Hands on Steering Wheel: One **OR** *Two*

In Car: Air-Conditioning **OR** *Open Window*

■ ■ ■

Convertible **OR** *Hard Top*

■ ■ ■

Travel Half Mile: Walk **OR** *Drive*

■ ■ ■

White Car **OR** *Black Car*

■ ■ ■

Quarter Tank: Get Gas **OR**
Wait Till Nearly Empty

■ ■ ■

Lease **OR** *Own*

Used Car **OR** *New Car*

■   ■   ■

Porsche **OR** *Jaguar*

■   ■   ■

Edsel **OR** *DeLorean*

■   ■   ■

Mercedes **OR** *BMW*

■   ■   ■

Travel to Airport: Stretch Limo **OR** *Cab*

■   ■   ■

Car Repair: Dealership **OR** *Gas Station*

■   ■   ■

Carsick **OR** *Airsick*

Silent Burglar Alarm **OR** *Kill Switch*

■ ■ ■

Lojack **OR** *The Club*

■ ■ ■

First Car: Parents Pay **OR** *Kids Pay*

■ ■ ■

1959 Cadillac **OR** *1957 Thunderbird*

■ ■ ■

Henry Ford **OR** *Lee Iacocca*

■ ■ ■

Volkswagen Beetle: Old **OR** *New*

■ ■ ■

Lost: Ask for Help **OR** *Wing It*

Rolls-Royce **OR** Bentley

■ ■ ■

Winter: All-Weather Tires **OR** Snow Tires

■ ■ ■

Obey Speed Limit **OR** Fudge a Little

■ ■ ■

Motor Home **OR** Houseboat

■ ■ ■

Driver **OR** Passenger

■ ■ ■

Passenger: Shotgun **OR** Backseat

■ ■ ■

Motorcycle **OR** Moped

Cadillac DeVille **OR** *Lincoln Continental*

■ ■ ■

Matchbox **OR** *Hot Wheels*

■ ■ ■

Lost, No Map, Fork in Road, Go:
Left **OR** *Right*

■ ■ ■

License Plate:
DMV-Issued **OR** *Vanity Plate*

■ ■ ■

Front-Wheel Drive **OR** *Rear-Wheel Drive*

■ ■ ■

Bumper Sticker **OR** *Fuzzy Dice*

On Window:

"Baby on Board" Sign **OR** *Garfield*

■ ■ ■

Pigeon in Road: Stop **OR** *Speed Up*

■ ■ ■

In Store for Moment:

Double-Park **OR** *Look for Spot*

■ ■ ■

Minivan **OR** *Station Wagon*

■ ■ ■

Cassette Player **OR** *CD Player*

OR 254

Drive-In Movie:
Watch Flick OR Make Out

■ ■ ■

Better Drive-Through: Bank OR Fast Food

■ ■ ■

Feed Parking Meter OR Gamble

■ ■ ■

Car Registration:
In Glove Compartment OR Wallet

■ ■ ■

Model Car OR Model Plane

■ ■ ■

Used-Car Salesman OR Car Mechanic

First Class **OR** Coach

■　■　■

Sing in the Car **OR**
Pick Your Nose in the Car

■　■　■

Sports Car **OR** Pickup Truck

■　■　■

Compact Car **OR** Luxury Car

■　■　■

Hot-Air Balloon Ride **OR** Helicopter Ride

■　■　■

Airplane Luggage: Carry On **OR** Check In

Bow **OR** Stern

. . .

Hail Cab: Wave **OR** Whistle

. . .

Cruise Around the World **OR**
Cruise to Nowhere

. . .

Motorcycle: Honda **OR** Harley Davidson

. . .

Traffic Accident:
Rubberneck **OR** Move Along

. . .

Change a Flat Tire **OR** Change a Baby

Flight: Domestic **OR** *International*

■ ■ ■

Arrival **OR** *Departure*

■ ■ ■

Six Cylinder **OR** *Eight Cylinder*

■ ■ ■

Dent Another Car in Parking Lot, No
Witnesses: Drive Away **OR** *Leave Note*

■ ■ ■

4 A.M., Red Light, No One Coming:
Stop **OR** *Drive Through*

■ ■ ■

Bus **OR** *Taxi*

Gas Station: Full Serve **OR** Self-Serve

■ ■ ■

Travel Agent **OR** Priceline.com

■ ■ ■

Drive Friend to Airport **OR**
Help Friend Move

■ ■ ■

Move Cross-Country: Drive **OR** Fly

■ ■ ■

Chrysler PT Cruiser:
Throwback **OR** Throw It Back

Thinkers

OR

Deep Thoughts

Short Term **OR** *Long Term*

■ ■ ■

Before **OR** *After*

■ ■ ■

Now **OR** *Later*

■ ■ ■

Maximum **OR** *Minimum*

■ ■ ■

July **OR** *January*

■ ■ ■

Hot **OR** *Cold*

■ ■ ■

Few **OR** *Many*

Saturday **OR** *Sunday*

∎ ∎ ∎

Noon **OR** *Midnight*

∎ ∎ ∎

Abortion **OR** *Adoption*

∎ ∎ ∎

Old **OR** *New*

∎ ∎ ∎

Black **OR** *White*

∎ ∎ ∎

Up **OR** *Down*

∎ ∎ ∎

On **OR** *Off*

Spring OR *Fall*

■ ■ ■

Daylight Saving Time OR *Standard Time*

■ ■ ■

Fire OR *Water*

■ ■ ■

Over OR *Under*

■ ■ ■

In OR *Out*

■ ■ ■

Long OR *Short*

■ ■ ■

Give OR *Receive*

Why **OR** *Why Not*

■　■　■

More **OR** *Less*

■　■　■

21st Century **OR** *25th Century*

■　■　■

Loud **OR** *Quiet*

■　■　■

Front **OR** *Back*

■　■　■

Thirsty **OR** *Hungry*

■　■　■

Two's Company **OR** *Three's a Crowd*

Clockwise **OR** *Counterclockwise*

■ ■ ■

The Center **OR** *The Edge*

■ ■ ■

P.O.W. **OR** *M.I.A.*

■ ■ ■

Yin **OR** *Yang*

■ ■ ■

Deaf **OR** *Blind*

■ ■ ■

Enlightenment **OR** *Ignorance*

■ ■ ■

Hammer **OR** *Nail*

Feed a Cold and Starve a Fever **OR**

Starve a Cold and Feed a Fever

■ ■ ■

Human Race's Greatest Achievement:

Democracy **OR** *Remote Control*

■ ■ ■

Nietzsche **OR** *St. Augustine*

■ ■ ■

Reincarnation **OR** *Heaven*

■ ■ ■

Known **OR** *The Unknown*

■ ■ ■

Win Lottery **OR** *Win Nobel Prize*

Give Donation to:

Organized Charity **OR** *Homeless Person*

■ ■ ■

Adult **OR** *Child*

■ ■ ■

Firing Squad **OR** *Hanging*

■ ■ ■

Cancer **OR** *Hit by Bus*

■ ■ ■

Widow **OR** *Divorcée*

■ ■ ■

For **OR** *Against*

Happy Birthday **OR** *Happy Anniversary*

■ ■ ■

Dishonorable Discharge **OR** *Section 8*

■ ■ ■

1950s **OR** *1990s*

■ ■ ■

Nervous Breakdown **OR** *Amnesia*

■ ■ ■

Big **OR** *Little*

■ ■ ■

On Call for Jury Duty **OR**
Watch Grass Grow

Hard **OR** *Soft*

■   ■   ■

Freud **OR** *Jung*

■   ■   ■

Thick **OR** *Thin*

■   ■   ■

Fast **OR** *Slow*

■   ■   ■

Commerce **OR** *Environment*

■   ■   ■

Net **OR** *Gross*

■   ■   ■

Lose: Memory **OR** *Hair*

Open **OR** Close

∎ ∎ ∎

Green **OR** Brown

∎ ∎ ∎

Nearsighted **OR** Farsighted

∎ ∎ ∎

Burial **OR** Cremation

∎ ∎ ∎

Guilty: Plea Bargain **OR**
Go to Trial and Take Chances

∎ ∎ ∎

Handwriting Analysis:
Telling **OR** Tells Nothing

Ghosts: Exist OR
Not a Ghost of a Chance

■ ■ ■

Human Cloning:
Improves Society OR *Mutates Society*

■ ■ ■

Hypnotism: Fact OR *Fiction*

■ ■ ■

Tarot Cards:
Hocus-Pocus OR *Revealing*

■ ■ ■

Transcendental Mediation OR *Zen*

Day **OR** *Night*

■ ■ ■

Give Speech: First **OR** *Last*

■ ■ ■

No Food or Rest in 48 Hours:
Sleep First **OR** *Eat First*

■ ■ ■

Loved One Dying:
Pull the Plug **OR** *Hope for the Best*

■ ■ ■

Circle **OR** *Square*

Triangle OR *Rectangle*

■ ■ ■

Consensus OR *Individuality*

■ ■ ■

Honesty Is the Best Policy:
Truth OR *Lie*

■ ■ ■

Yes OR *No*

■ ■ ■

Rather Be in:

Who's Who in America OR

Guinness Book of World Records

Can Only Save One Drowning Loved One,

Rescue: Spouse **OR** *Child*

■ ■ ■

Money **OR** *Intelligence*

■ ■ ■

Nostradamus **OR** *Confucius*

■ ■ ■

Mostly Cloudy **OR** *Partly Sunny*

■ ■ ■

Stay **OR** *Go*

■ ■ ■

Early **OR** *Late*

This

OR

That

Pyromaniac **OR** *Kleptomaniac*

■　■　■

Beagle **OR** *Poodle*

■　■　■

Daisy **OR** *Daffodil*

■　■　■

Asleep **OR** *Awake*

■　■　■

Crocodile **OR** *Alligator*

■　■　■

Yellow Pages **OR** *White Pages*

■　■　■

Pets **OR** *Plants*

This OR That

Paper Clip **OR** *Staple*

. . .

Cigar **OR** *Pipe*

. . .

Cross Out **OR** *Erase*

. . .

Groundhog Day **OR** *Arbor Day*

. . .

Friends **OR** *Family*

. . .

Isn't **OR** *Ain't*

. . .

Bellybutton: Innie **OR** *Outie*

Emerald **OR** Pearl

∎ ∎ ∎

Attend Mass:
Christmas Eve **OR** Christmas Day

∎ ∎ ∎

Open Christmas Presents:
Christmas Eve **OR** Christmas Day

∎ ∎ ∎

Blood Bank **OR** Sperm Bank

∎ ∎ ∎

Kiwanis **OR** Knights of Columbus

∎ ∎ ∎

Cough **OR** Sneeze

Motel **OR** *Hotel*

■ ■ ■

April Fool's Day **OR** *Halloween*

■ ■ ■

Brand Name **OR** *Generic*

■ ■ ■

Return Address: Upper Left **OR** *Back Flap*

■ ■ ■

Scab: Pick **OR** *Heal*

■ ■ ■

Bookmark **OR** *Fold Page*

■ ■ ■

Print **OR** *Script*

Stamp Collector **OR** *Coin Collector*

■ ■ ■

New Year's Eve: Go Out **OR** *Stay Home*

■ ■ ■

Tonsillectomy **OR** *Appendectomy*

■ ■ ■

Bottles and Cans:
City Recycling **OR** *Return for Deposit*

■ ■ ■

Baby Boomer **OR** *Generation X*

■ ■ ■

Hang Nail **OR** *Splinter*

Typing: Hunt and Peck **OR** *Use Home Keys*

■   ■   ■

Pet: Bird **OR** *Fish*

■   ■   ■

Moving: U-Haul **OR** *Hire Movers*

■   ■   ■

Knock-Kneed **OR** *Bow-Legged*

■   ■   ■

Screwdriver: Flathead **OR** *Phillips*

■   ■   ■

Bar Graph **OR** *Pie Chart*

■   ■   ■

Shetland Pony **OR** *Clydesdale*

Parrot **OR** *Canary*

■　■　■

Pet: Spay **OR** *Breed*

■　■　■

Bed & Breakfast **OR** *Five-Star Hotel*

■　■　■

Metric System in America:
Will Never Catch On **OR** *Long Overdue*

■　■　■

Friendly Correspondence:
Phone Call **OR** *Write Letter*

■　■　■

Tulips **OR** *Roses*

Photos: Glossy **OR** *Matte Finish*

∎ ∎ ∎

Blow Up Balloon: Helium **OR** *Lungs*

∎ ∎ ∎

Christmas Shopping:
Day After Thanksgiving **OR** *December 24*

∎ ∎ ∎

Sleep: One Pillow **OR** *Two Pillows*

∎ ∎ ∎

Tag/Garage Sale **OR**
Flea Market/Swap Meet

∎ ∎ ∎

Sun **OR** *Shade*

Neck Pain **OR** *Back Pain*

■ ■ ■

Two-Year Old, $20 Blender Broken:
Repair **OR** *Replace*

■ ■ ■

Greeting Card: Sentimental **OR** *Funny*

■ ■ ■

Cockroach **OR** *Rat*

■ ■ ■

Quit Smoking: Patch **OR** *Cold Turkey*

■ ■ ■

Hold Dustpan **OR** *Sweep*

Pet Owner on Vacation:

Hire Pet-Sitter **OR** *Board at Kennel*

. . .

Aging Sick Pet:

Pull the Plug **OR** *Keep Alive*

. . .

Handshake **OR** *Soul Shake*

. . .

Aquarius **OR** *Scorpio*

. . .

Hippopotamus **OR** *Rhinoceros*

Tortoise **OR** *Hare*

■ ■ ■

Bill Clinton's Pet: Socks **OR** *Buddy*

■ ■ ■

Dog Owners: Use Pooper-Scooper **OR**
It's a Natural Fertilizer

■ ■ ■

Perfer to Be Called by:
Nickname **OR** *Real Name*

■ ■ ■

At Front Door:
Knock **OR** *Use Doorbell*

Threesomes

OR

Three's a Crowd

Chocolate **OR** *Vanilla* **OR** *Strawberry*

■ ■ ■

Tea with: *Lemon* **OR** *Milk* **OR** *Sugar*

■ ■ ■

Republican **OR** *Democrat* **OR** *Independent*

■ ■ ■

Larry **OR** *Moe* **OR** *Curly*

■ ■ ■

Kukla **OR** *Fran* **OR** *Ollie*

■ ■ ■

Blond **OR** *Brunette* **OR** *Redhead*

■ ■ ■

Rock **OR** *Paper* **OR** *Scissors*

Breakfast OR *Lunch* OR *Dinner*

■ ■ ■

Nightly News: ABC OR *NBC* OR *CBS*

■ ■ ■

Knife OR *Fork* OR *Spoon*

■ ■ ■

Heat: Gas OR *Electric* OR *Oil*

■ ■ ■

Meat: Rare OR *Medium* OR *Well Done*

■ ■ ■

Orthodox OR *Conservative* OR *Reform*

■ ■ ■

Blinds OR *Curtains* OR *Shutters*

Lions **OR** *Tigers* **OR** *Bears*

∎ ∎ ∎

Soda: Small **OR** *Medium* **OR** *Large*

∎ ∎ ∎

Plato **OR** *Aristotle* **OR** *Socrates*

∎ ∎ ∎

Sugar **OR** *Equal* **OR** *Sweet & Low*

∎ ∎ ∎

Peter **OR** *Paul* **OR** *Mary*

∎ ∎ ∎

Punt **OR** *Pass* **OR** *Kick*

∎ ∎ ∎

Sleep: Stomach **OR** *Side* **OR** *Back*

Hear No Evil **OR**
See No Evil **OR** *Speak No Evil*

■ ■ ■

Bobby Unser **OR**
Al Unser **OR** *Al Unser, Jr.*

■ ■ ■

Faith **OR** *Hope* **OR** *Charity*

■ ■ ■

Jeff Bridges **OR** *Beau Bridges*
OR *Lloyd Bridges*

■ ■ ■

Hercules **OR** *Sampson* **OR**
The Incredible Hulk

Take Work Home OR Work Late
OR Leave Work for Next Day

■ ■ ■

The Three Little Pigs OR The Three Tenors
OR The Three Amigos

■ ■ ■

A Box of Biscuits OR A Box of Mixed
Biscuits OR A Biscuit Mixer

■ ■ ■

Pushups OR Chinups OR Situps

■ ■ ■

Judiciary OR Legislative OR Executive

Planes OR *Trains* OR *Automobiles*

∎ ∎ ∎

PGA Tour OR *LPGA Tour*
OR *Senior Tour*

∎ ∎ ∎

Batman: Michael Keaton OR
George Clooney OR *Val Kilmer*

∎ ∎ ∎

Groucho Marx OR *Harpo Marx*
OR *Chico Marx*

∎ ∎ ∎

Win OR *Place* OR *Show*

Pillow: Feathered OR

Foam Rubber OR *Buckwheat*

■ ■ ■

Twins OR *Triplets* OR *Quadruplets*

■ ■ ■

Henry Fonda OR *Jane Fonda*

OR *Peter Fonda*

■ ■ ■

Elba OR *Devil's Island* OR *Alcatraz*

■ ■ ■

Suez Canal OR *Erie Canal*

OR *Panama Canal*

UPS **OR** *FedEx*
OR *U.S. Postal Service*

■ ■ ■

Yesterday **OR** *Today* **OR** *Tomorrow*

■ ■ ■

Snap **OR** *Crackle* **OR** *Pop*

■ ■ ■

Yours **OR** *Mine* **OR** *Ours*

■ ■ ■

Ron Howard's Legacy: Opie **OR**
Richie Cunningham **OR** *Director*

The Cowardly Lion **OR** *The Tin Man*
OR *The Scarecrow*

■ ■ ■

Let's Make a Deal: *Door #1*
OR *Door #2* **OR** *Door #3*

■ ■ ■

General Motors **OR** *Ford* **OR** *Chrysler*

■ ■ ■

Gary Coleman **OR** *Todd Bridges*
OR *Dana Plato*

■ ■ ■

Animal **OR** *Vegetable* **OR** *Mineral*

Solid **OR** *Liquid* **OR** *Gas*

■ ■ ■

Jimmy Smits **OR** *David Caruso*
OR *Rick Schroder*

■ ■ ■

Bow Tie **OR** *Necktie* **OR** *Bolo*

■ ■ ■

Sleep Attire: Pajamas **OR**
Underwear **OR** *Nude*

■ ■ ■

Hop **OR** *Skip* **OR** *Jump*

James Bond: Roger Moore OR
Sean Connery OR *Pierce Brosnan*

■ ■ ■

Pencil: #1 OR *#2* OR *#3*

■ ■ ■

School Shootings: Kids' Fault
OR *Parents' Fault* OR *Society's Fault*

■ ■ ■

Favorite Primary Color:
Red OR *Yellow* OR *Blue*

Scotch Tape **OR** *Glue* **OR** *Paste*

∎ ∎ ∎

Pokémon Characters:
Pikachu **OR** *Jigglypuff* **OR** *Bulbasaur*

∎ ∎ ∎

Chocolate: Dark **OR** *Milk* **OR** *White*

∎ ∎ ∎

Present **OR** *Past* **OR** *Future*

∎ ∎ ∎

AT&T **OR** *Sprint* **OR** *Worldcom*

Famous

OR

Historical ORs

Note: This list recognizes two choices often associated with each other. It is not necessary to pick one or the other. However, can you state where these sayings or phrases originated? Don't know? Be creative.

Give Me Liberty **OR** Give Me Death

■　■　■

To Be **OR** Not to Be

■　■　■

California **OR** Bust

■　■　■

Friend **OR** Foe

■　■　■

Wanted: Dead **OR** Alive

■　■　■

Sink **OR** Swim

■　■　■

Guilty **OR** Not Guilty

Open with Jacks **OR** *Better*

∎   ∎   ∎

Take It **OR** *Leave It*

∎   ∎   ∎

Pay Me Now **OR** *Pay Me Later*

∎   ∎   ∎

Do **OR** *Die*

∎   ∎   ∎

Is It Live **OR** *Is It Memorex*

∎   ∎   ∎

Thumbs Up **OR** *Thumbs Down*

∎   ∎   ∎

Your Money **OR** *Your Life*

Eye Doctor to Patient:
Is It Better This Way **OR** *This Way*

■ ■ ■

For Richer **OR** *For Poorer*

■ ■ ■

For Better **OR** *For Worse*

■ ■ ■

Move It **OR** *Lose It*

■ ■ ■

Is That a Gun in Your Pocket **OR**
Are You Just Glad to See Me

■ ■ ■

Hit **OR** *Miss*

Six of One **OR** *A Half Dozen of Another*

■ ■ ■

Rock **OR** *A Hard Place*

■ ■ ■

True **OR** *False*

■ ■ ■

By Hook **OR** *By Crook*

■ ■ ■

Be Good **OR** *Else*

■ ■ ■

Hell **OR** *High Water*

■ ■ ■

Be There **OR** *Be Square*

Personalized
OR
Custom-made ORs

Now that you've absorbed the concept of the book, it might be fun putting your own ORs together. Expand upon the list of ORs from chapters already in the book or branch out on your own.

For example, we've all had unique experiences and adventures to which only you, and maybe those who are close to you, can relate. Also, only you know about your crazy aunt or irascible uncle. Try matching them up and see which one you pick.

On the following page create your own tailor-made OR list.

Tell us about your ORs
at www.orbook.com.

Afterword

"Now when all the souls had chosen their lives they went in the order of their lots to Lachesis; and she gave each into the charge of the guardian genius he had chosen, to escort him through life and fulfill his choice."

—PLATO, *THE REPUBLIC*, CHAPTER X, "THE MYTH OF ER"

OR

"It ain't over till it's over."

—YOGI BERRA